Black, Brilliant
and Dyslexic

of related interest

Dyslexia and Me
Surviving and Thriving as a Neurodivergent Entrepreneur
Onyinye Udokporo
ISBN 978 1 78775 944 2
eISBN 978 1 78775 945 9

The Adult Side of Dyslexia
Kelli Sandman-Hurley
ISBN 978 1 78775 475 1
eISBN 978 1 78775 476 8

**The Bigger Picture Book of Amazing
Dyslexics and the Jobs They Do**
Kathy Iwanczak Forsyth and Kate Power
Foreword by Paul Smith
ISBN 978 1 78592 584 9
eISBN 978 1 78592 585 6

Creative, Successful, Dyslexic
23 High Achievers Share Their Stories
Margaret Rooke
Foreword by Mollie King
ISBN 978 1 84905 653 3
eISBN 978 1 78450 163 1

The Illustrated Guide to Dyslexia and Its Amazing People
Kate Power & Kathy Iwanczak Forsyth
Foreword by Richard Rogers
ISBN 978 1 78592 330 2
eISBN 978 1 78450 647 6

Dyslexia Advocate!
How to Advocate for a Child with Dyslexia
within the Public Education System
Kelli Sandman-Hurley
ISBN 978 1 84905 737 0
eISBN 978 1 78450 274 4

Black, Brilliant and Dyslexic

Neurodivergent Heroes Tell their Stories

Edited by Marcia Brissett-Bailey

Foreword by Atif Choudhury

Jessica Kingsley Publishers
London and Philadelphia

First published in Great Britain in 2023 by Jessica Kingsley Publishers
An imprint of Hodder & Stoughton Ltd
An Hachette UK Company

2

The fonts, layout and overall design of this book have been prepared
according to dyslexia friendly principles. At JKP we aim to make our
books' content accessible to as many readers as possible.

**Content warning: This book mentions anxiety, bullying
and mental health.**

A CIP catalogue record for this title is available from the
British Library and the Library of Congress

ISBN 978 1 83997 133 4
eISBN 978 1 83997 134 1

Printed and bound in the United States by Integrated
Books International

Jessica Kingsley Publishers' policy is to use papers that are natural,
renewable and recyclable products and made from wood grown
in sustainable forests. The logging and manufacturing processes
are expected to conform to the environmental regulations
of the country of origin.

Jessica Kingsley Publishers
Carmelite House
50 Victoria Embankment
London EC4Y 0DZ

www.jkp.com

I dedicate this book to four phenomenal and influential women in my life: my mum Ann-Marie Bennett, for fighting for me at school; my mum's mum Granny Eliza Rebecca Scott (and my second mum, also known as Ms Scott), for her wisdom; Dolcie Brissett (Mamma, my dad's mum), for her love and providing meaning to the word family, which was felt all the way from Jamaica to the UK; and my auntie Gloria, for her unconditional love. They enabled me to understand my roots, culture and identity and to live as a black woman, with no apologies.

I also want to acknowledge my ancestors, creator/God and guardian angels, known and unknown, for their guidance and for listening to me and giving me the strength when I did not believe in me and did not feel good enough.

Mum and Dad, you have been instrumental by showing me nothing but love and believing in my goals and aspirations to reach my full potential and be the best version of me.

Contents

"As a proud black dyslexic woman, I am really pleased to see the issue of dyslexia in the black community discussed further and consciousness raised about so many people's experiences.

Asher Hoyles, learning support practitioner, author and performance poet.

Foreword

When we are not Intersectional, we are not relevant; this is a value as well as a shared question, one I've demanded of myself and the Diversity and Ability[1] team since the day we began. We've grown to redress this issue, re-examine its meaning and  allow its unlocked reality to reshape aspirations. As a result, we've found ourselves on intrepid journeys and have shared aspirations, as well as fear. It is here we remain relentless.

---

1   Diversity and Ability (diversityandability.com) is a multi-award-winning social enterprise, led by and for disabled people. At Diversity and Ability, the mission is to inform and advocate for intersectional neurodiversity and disability inclusion through technology, training and talent. It recognizes the strength and value of lived experience, celebrating the voices of disabled and neurodiverse people with the aim of creating a world in which everyone can participate and thrive.

We recognize that none of us is defined by the convenience of simple labels, especially ones that other people give us.

Marcia Brissett-Bailey is a companion on this journey, a sojourner, finding a voice and seeking to support the voices of countless others – Black and Asian voices previously silenced through their differences. Curiosity to understand social injustice and structural racism is where this journey starts. Without the options of choice, it's where we both began. Just as all people of colour who come from marginalized experiences, we come in search of community, familiarity and belonging. At times, we battle shame, we reignite pride and occasionally reassure ourselves enough to accept the differences we can't hide and learn to live with those we can. But in truth, this is no answer. In truth, disabled and neurodiverse people of colour come, not in search of reasonable adjustments, but rather, in search of safety. In truth, we do not seek to apologize for our differences, but instead strive to hear harmony and search longingly for a place where differences aren't just accommodated but are needed and valued. Never is this more true than in the lives of neurodiverse, socio-economically deprived Black children.

In an already imbalanced world, perception and ingenuity are anonymous gifts, uncharted maps showing us accessible roads home, yet how rarely a civil society picks these maps up. And as a consequence, we all remain lost...

How can we justify that Black people are more than four times as likely as white people to be detained under the Mental

Health Act?[2] And how can we fathom the disproportionate overrepresentation of Black and ethnic minority groups in the criminal justice system? People of minority ethnicities make up 27 per cent of the prison population compared with 13 per cent of the general population (Sturge 2021). Meanwhile, half of those entering prison could reasonably be expected to be neurodiverse (*Neurodiversity in the Criminal Justice System: A Review of Evidence* 2021). So, if we cross-reference these known facts, we may deduce that Black neurodiverse people are among the most excluded, marginalized groups in our society.

Offering solidarity to neurodiverse people facing learning isolation as they navigate exclusion is an act of justice. It is intricately rooted in historical wrongdoings and can be received as a form of reparation. Unspoken and yet felt daily, recognitions of the post-slavery world are structural traumas to be healed. The trauma of European imperialism, educational demands and a language commanded and taught down the barrel of a gun continues to echo for generations.

This book, *Black, Brilliant and Dyslexic* – call it anti-racism in action, call it diversity, even call it dangerous, call it what you will – should be recognized, above all, as an urgent call to do better.

---

2 Black people were most likely to be detained under the Mental Health Act in the year to March 2019, with 321.7 detentions per 100,000 people. Figure taken from: www.ethnicity-facts-figures. service.gov.uk/health/mental-health/detentions-under-the-mental-health-act/latest

As American writer and activist James Baldwin once said, 'not everything we face can be changed, but nothing can be changed until it is faced'. For children from ethnic minorities impacted by dyslexia, social exclusion and learning isolation is an injustice and represents a loss to us all. Yes, it is hard to collectively face, but face it we must. As Marcia and I discovered, our shared experience of coping at school by choosing to be selectively mute led us to realize that the silence of children is expensive; it robs us all. When children repress their voices, a society loses innovation, it loses laughter and, sometimes, it permanently loses participation. This can be heart-wrenching to comprehend and yet civil society must be compelled to register it. The impact for millions remains devastating. Wounded children become wounded adults.

As a friend, a leader, a father, a chief executive and a Bengali man growing up in social poverty with dyslexia, I am grateful for the intimacy and the boldness in which Marcia has worked the principles she advocates and the conversations we've had. It is said that there is so much wisdom in the stories women never tell. As a mother, a dyslexia campaigner, an author, a career guidance champion, she is a joy to be around and her work for genuine change is infectious. So, I am grateful to Marcia and all who have contributed so willingly to this book, for the wisdom they've shared and the stories they've decided to tell. This is what diversity of thought can do. This is social advocacy at its best, born out of lived experiences. This book speaks to the heart of intersectional relevance. This is the gift. An emotional labour given with love and learned through pain, this gift is not to be taken lightly, so learn, unlearn and relearn as we build a new and relevant journey of inclusion together. When welcomed, diversity of thought can truly change the world; perhaps it's the only thing that ever does.

——

Atif Choudhury, Chief Executive, Diversity and Ability.

Acknowledgements

Many special people have been part of my book journey and in life, and I'd like to thank them.

Thank you to my children, Ayana and Omari, for your understanding of mummy's constant engagement with her laptop; to Brian, my husband, for your support throughout my book journey. To Linda Derby, my soul sister, I value your support and your time in writing up many of the transcripts from interviews with contributors to this book. To my sisters, Keyonta Brissett for her creative lens, and Treena Hall and Cheryle Martin-Mckie, and to my bestie Sian Lord-Baptiste for just being you, and to my brothers. To Asher Hoyles, who raised my consciousness of dyslexia from a cultural perspective when you asked me to be in your book, unknowing of the power it would give to me in finding my voice. To my coach and friend, Jannett Morgan, there are no words but 'thank you'. To my accountability buddy, Patricia Bidi, for our 7am meetings during our book journey, and to Tara Martin for all the photo editing. I must not forget the Queendom Academy sisters, Neusa Catoja, Lorna Archer and Michelle Harding, for their 21 Days of Abundance support.

ACKNOWLEDGEMENTS

People who have been instrumental in my book journey
include Margaret Rooke, for her mentorship, as well as
Julian Bond, for support at the beginning. To Joanna Oliver,
who is a light of wisdom, connecting the dots at the end
of my book journey, with all her editing and proofreading
of this book, gratitude always – we all have strengths and
I thank you for yours. Thank you also to Liz Gentilcore and
Atif Choudhury; I value and appreciate your insight and
knowledge in reviewing this book, bringing in the perspective
of other professionals and from the lived experiences of other
neurodiverse voices.

Dyslexia and neurodiversity family and community

Special thanks to a few people:

First, to Jennifer (Jenny) Machwhinnie, you provided me with
butterfly wings and with strategies to learn how to fly. You
believed in me and empowered me to support my progression
and passion for learning, as well as enabling me to find my
voice, so I no longer felt stupid.

To my master's support tutor, Penny Speller, you were worth
your weight in gold; you told me during my research paper,
'Marcia you're writing for a PhD, not an MA', and that made
see my potential even more – thank you.

To Kate and Kathy, from Amazing Dyslexics and all trustees of
Waltham Forest Dyslexia Association, for your moral support,

especially the WFDA community for your words of wisdom; I am truly grateful. To Nancy Doyle for giving the platform to feature in Forbes, amplifying neurodiverse voices, and for your friendship. I did not realize the impact, journey and opportunities it would bring and the people I would meet from around the world. To Charles Freeman, Keisha Adair Swaby and Karinna Brown-Williams and Winsome Duncan, for creating the opportunity to be an author, first with Peaches Publications and Pioneering Women Speak. To the original members of the British Dyslexia Association Cultural Perspective Committee, including co-founder Joseline Porter, Ruth-Ellen Danquah, Leslie Lewis-Walker, Lucita ComWillis-Paul and Zoe-Jane Littlewood, for being supportive in this process. Another part of my neurodiverse family also includes Indigo Evolve, Homecoming Project, Remi Ray, Tumi Sotire and Lorna Cadogan; catch-up groups – Karen, Yvonne and Racheal and my sister-friends and colleagues from Newham Sixth Form College days, working as a careers advisor, and Dionne, Sally, Diana and Henrietta. Thank you to Pamela R Haynes and Grace Graham, for your support and kind words of advice and mentoring.

I feel blessed that I have a tribe and community of positive people who believe in me, empower and encourage me to stretch my personal growth and support my ideas, enabling me to dare to dream and achieve my goals, judgement free. How precious to have friendship in which I can feel belonging, without explanation, and can be my best version of me.

To all 26 contributors to this book and those who have

provided quotes to the book...thank you for trusting this process. Gratitude always.

Thank you to Amy Lankester-Owen, for seeing my vision and taking my proposal, to the opportunity and the panel at Jessica Kingsley Publishers (JKP), and also to Isabel Martin and Abbie Howard – everyone needs a go-to person and you have both been amazing editorial assistants.

Acknowledgement to my family, especially my mum and dad, for your unconditional love and always believing in me and supporting my dreams with words of encouragement.

Finally, thanks to all who do not judge someone, whatever the problem, before they know the abilities of the person concerned.

Introduction

Black, Brilliant and Dyslexic is a raw account of the lives of black people with dyslexia; taking an intercultural perspective of people ranging from UK, US and African and Caribbean birth/heritage. It charts journeys from early childhood, through the education system, to adulthood and subsequent workplace and everyday life, illustrating how black men, women and young people who are dyslexic and neurodivergent are changing the world, even though they are hardly represented within the public arena.

To compound this, there may be a reluctance within sections of the black community to consider that children and adults may be dyslexic, as neurodiverse learning differences can be viewed as shameful, even as something that can be reversed by 'hard work'. Parents may resist the perceived 'white label' of dyslexia being given to their children. You will hear stories of this in the book, from individuals not understanding and dismissing dyslexia as something made up to put their child down, along with all the other labels they're being given.

Being misunderstood and labelled is one thing but the worst

of all, for me, is people thinking they know who you are, based on a lack of information and literature.

I am a black woman with dyslexia and it is vital that I always bring my own perspective, from my upbringing and lived experience. I share a commonality with many black people but I am still an individual and authentically me by design. I never intended to be a spokesperson for equality and inclusion, I share the experiences of discrimination with many contributors in the book, and I felt compelled to speak out and provide a platform for others.

Atif Choudhury, Chief Executive of Diversity and Ability, who wrote the Foreword for this book, really touches the core root by saying, 'We are all neurodiverse, we're just not all marginalized by it.'

To me, it brings awareness but my intention in life was never to talk about inequalities. However, from the moment I was born, I feel that I was a statistic waiting to happen, due to being born to a teenage mum, the colour of my skin and my limited opportunities to learn within an education system which created intersectional and systematic barriers.

It became exhausting, and I experienced burnout as a result of having to always fight my corner in order to reach my potential, feeling invisible and being excluded from society due to the colour of my skin, my gender and my disability.

Intersectionality is a term created by Dr Kimberlé Crenshaw

to describe the experience of living with multiple identities of gender, race, culture, disability, gender identity, sexual orientation and immigration status. This notion of 'multiple identity' resonates strongly for me. The complexity of dyslexia shows that it is authentically unique, like a fingerprint, and no one person is the same and we can have overlapping traits of other neurodiverse learning differences. I would also say that intersectional identity can have an impact on each person's profile, which can include factors such as race, education, class and environment, and this has been my own experience and also that of some who have shared their stories in this book.

Another demonstration of this reality can be seen in publicized government statistics. For example, among the five broad ethnic groups, known rates of detention under the Mental Health Act for the 'Black or Black British' group (321.7 detentions per 100,000 population) were over four times those of the white group (73.4 per 100,000 population) (see footnote 2 in Foreword). This is a prime example of how intersectionality in healthcare affects the level of care received by the Black community. Neurodiverse conditions such as autism or attention deficit hyperactivity disorder (ADHD) often go hand in hand with other mental health conditions, such as anxiety and depression, yet this link is often overlooked.

There is a distinct lack of dedicated resources, cultural literature and research available to black and marginalized communities regarding health, disability and education, and this goes hand-in-hand with the lack of awareness and acceptance as there is not enough representation in the media to change the narrative and normalize black dyslexia and neurodiversity, which I feel is so important to put out there, as the narrative needs to change (Blakis 2021).

Dyslexia can be diagnosed at primary school age, right into adulthood. Some contributors to this book were fortunate to be diagnosed with dyslexia at an early age and were able to get the right support in place at school, while some of us were totally missed and struggled through the education system that was meant to nurture and support our learning. Many in this book were only diagnosed at university, and those who did not go to university found out much later in their working life. There will be many stories untold due to not having a diagnosis; this book is just a snippet, and I am truly mindful that there are many people navigating silently in the world of words, with no voice to express their authentic self, instead feeling frustrated, lonely and scared. I feel and see you and this book is for you too.

When I was growing up, It seemed as if dyslexia only existed within a very white middle-class context. Even now it appears to have been hijacked by what feels like an elitist white male and, in more rare instances, white female section of the population.

Talking about black and dyslexic experience in the same sentence can almost feel as if I have said a bad word.

This is why it's so important to allow black people to tell their stories and express themselves in a book that's written for their communities, as well as to educate others who may consciously or unconsciously possess racist attitudes. There needs to be a shift in thinking and awareness of the barriers affecting people within the black and diverse dyslexic community.

We only need to look at the publications and social platforms of most dyslexia or neurodiversity organizations to see that they have a Eurocentric or white-American perspective. This includes boards of trustees selected for their expertise, but which lack diversity and an understanding of cultural literacy, environment, class, race, education and social barriers. This leads to a lack of representation of different cultural perspectives in the books and publications about dyslexia.

The issue of black people with dyslexia therefore takes us into the world of institutional racism and intersectional obstacles.

The workplace and educational institutions need to establish more transparent, simple, yet formal processes and to investigate discrimination on grounds of disability and race. Equality and inclusion should be a high priority but I feel still it is largely based on assumptions of what an individual would benefit from. Equality should seek to engage with individuals to understand their lived experience and to value and nurture belonging, participation, access to opportunities and equity, to lift people up so they can learn, grow and adapt. All these approaches are necessary to create a more equal society for those most marginalized.

When interviewing contributors for this book, I came across black dyslexic people who had left careers, as they did not feel they culturally belonged, but such companies as they worked for are missing out on talent and opportunities to create an enriched, diverse organization. Other issues which seemed to come up for several of the contributors to this book, and may be being experienced more widely, include black dyslexic people feeling as if they have to work at least twice as hard as everyone else; learning differences like dyslexia and dyspraxia being misunderstood as 'diseases' or taboo in some cultures and communities; and black children in schools being encouraged in sports but not having their dyslexia recognized in the academic realm, and therefore not receiving the necessary support in the classroom. What is heartening to see is that the younger contributors described situations where they were getting diagnosed earlier and having supports put in place, which suggests things may perhaps be changing slowly.

This book aims to raise awareness in the black and dyslexic communities at large, in order to break the silence, tackle the stigma surrounding dyslexia and address the barriers that hinder its disclosure, particularly among black people. As a 'hidden' learning difference, dyslexia can too often go unnoticed and may be disguised as something else.

There is a lack of data related to intersectional diversity, which would help us to understand more about the interplay between neurodiversity and other aspects of identity.

I feel so humbled to have been featured at the beginning of 'black dyslexic lived experience and voices' in Asher and Martin Hoyles' book, *Dyslexia from a Cultural Perspective*, carrying the baton on to *Black, Brilliant and Dyslexic.* It's so vital to hear our stories, and I have nothing but gratitude for the contributors who share their lived experience in this book, helping to challenge the tired old stereotypes of what dyslexia looks like.

YES, black people can be dyslexic AND be successful too! I'm not saying that living with dyslexia daily (and for me, also ADHD traits) is easy though.

This book illustrates how the contributors have overcome adversity, while providing practical advice to help others to unapologetically own the intersection of their blackness and dyslexia. It provides visible role models, which are currently virtually non-existent, to highlight the challenges, progress, successes and contributions within the black, dyslexic community. This book exists to help children, young people and adults to feel empowered and find their voice, to seek the help they need and to be proud of the way their brain works differently. The world needs different kinds of thinkers!

I have learned to be kind to myself and I hope this book encourages this in others too.

This book is also for those who have been diagnosed, misdiagnosed or never diagnosed with dyslexia or neurodiversity and have had to navigate the education system, workplace and entrepreneurship. It is also for parents and educators to gain insight into lived experiences of people from the black and dyslexic community.

I am passionate about representation of dyslexia and neurodiversity, from a cultural perspective and so that individual voices are heard. Role models are important; when I was growing up, I never had people who were dyslexic and looked like me sharing their stories and lived experience. My book creates positive role models for brown and black people within our wider dyslexic community and society, to inspire a new generation.

About Dyslexia and Neurodiversity

What is dyslexia?

There is no one clear definition of dyslexia; it has been defined in different ways and I have come across over 35 definitions of dyslexia in my research! The complexity of dyslexia is that it is authentically unique, like a finger print. No two people are the same and we can have overlapping traits of other neurodiverse learning differences. As I said before, lived experience of dyslexia can include and be impacted by race, education, class and environment. I do not list these factors lightly but they have been my own experience and also that of some who have shared their experiences or quotes in this book.

Definitions that are commonly cited include those given by the World Federation of Neurology (1968, p.26) as 'a disorder manifested by difficulty in learning to read, despite conventional instruction, adequate intelligence and socio-cultural opportunity. It is dependent upon fundamental cognitive disabilities, which are frequently constitutional in origin'.

The British Dyslexia Association reports that dyslexia is a combination of abilities and difficulties that affect the learning process in one or more of reading, spelling and writing. Accompanying weaknesses may be identified in areas of speed of processing, short-term memory, organization, sequencing, spoken language and motor skills. There may be difficulties with auditory and/or visual perception. Dyslexia can occur despite normal intellectual ability and education opportunity. It is constitutional in origin, part of one's make-up and independent of socio-economic status.

Commonly, when people hear the word 'dyslexia' they think only of reading, writing and spelling problems a child is having in school, with no focus on adults or the accompanying emotional difficulties such as self-esteem. Some associate it with slow learners. Almost everyone considers it to be some form of learning disability, and there is hardly any focus on its strengths.

Dyslexia is defined as a neurological (rather than psychological or behavioural), which can run in families (genetic) and is universal, irrespective of intelligence, culture, gender or nationality (Illingworth 2005). Literacy itself is a complex, adaptive skill which uses a range of neurological functions and interacts with the style of language (e.g. the balance of sounds and images; think Chinese compared with English). Any one or more of the neurological functions required for literacy being compromised could cause difficulties here, which is why there is so much diversity among people with dyslexia. Chinese dyslexic brains look completely different from those of English-speaking dyslexic people (Opitz *et al.* 2014), for example. The original evolutionary purpose of the neurological function also needs to be considered – like memory, attention and pattern learning. However, there is evidence that these differences are not necessarily deficits and that compromises in one area of the brain are paired with strengths in others (von Károlyi *et al.* 2003). This subject is under-researched because as a society we have prized literacy as the route to success for over 150 years now.

The exact number of children or adults that have dyslexia is unknown. This is because of the fact that a lot of children are been assessed at a quite late age and sometimes they develop such good coping strategies that it makes it even harder for their teachers or parents to understand the problems. However, the British Dyslexia Association (BDA) estimates that in the western world, up to 10 per cent of children have some specific problems and about 4 per cent are severely affected (Smith 1993; Singleton 1996; BDA 2009). About two to four percent of the student population have dyslexia (Miles, 1991; Snowling, 1987 cited in Crombie, 1995). With such a prevalence, we have to ask ourselves if this neuro difference is truly an impairment and could in fact be an advantage in some situations. Surely there is a role for specialist thinking skills? This leads us to the neurodiversity movement.

What is neurodiversity?

The concept of neurodiversity is not new. Judy Singer, an

Australian sociologist, coined the term in the 1990s through online discussion and community work, with her early work focused on those with autism, particularly autistic adults, teens and parents. Many activists in the autistic community and beyond embrace the term. They and others, including myself, use it to reduce stigma and promote inclusion in education/training, the workplace and society.

Neurodiversity, like any diversity, is about difference: a brain wired differently that affects how the individual interacts and experiences the world. For some individuals, their neurodiversity may impair areas of their daily life, but their difference does not mean they are damaged. It says more about the inflexibility of the world than it does about us.

In understanding the definition, it is important for me to break down the concept of diversity. It is varied but it doesn't need to be complex and theoretical. My understanding is that each individual is unique and that we each recognize our individual differences. These can be along the dimensions of race, ethnicity, gender, sexual orientation, socio-economic factors, age, physical abilities, religious beliefs, or political or other ideologies.

It's also important to remember that there are several neurological differences, including: autism spectrum condition/disorder (ASC/D), attention deficit hyperactivity disorder (ADHD), dyslexia, dyspraxia/developmental co-ordination disorder (DCD), dyscalculia, dysgraphia, learning disability and Tourette syndrome, which are all recognized like any other human differences, such as gender and race.

According to ACAS, 'most people are neurotypical, meaning that their brain functions and processes information in the way society expects. However it is estimated that, around 1 in 7 people (more than 15% in the UK) are neurodivergent, meaning that the brains functions, learns and processes information differently'. These are often conditions that unless you or someone close to you have, you will have a limited understanding of and so you may not know how to embrace these differences. I can find no studies breaking this data down by race or ethnicity, so there is still more awareness and work to do in this area.

"The Black Dyslexic finds themselves in one of the most complicated states of being *the other*. Our skin, and all the social vulnerability that it carries, forces us to constantly assert our humanity. While our minds, which rarely find appropriate nurturing, can leave us feeling inadequate and invisible. From school to the world of work, we must cut through a tangle of stereotype threads to find our way to success. But there is beauty too. The Black Dyslexic can draw from the richness of our culture and the ingenuity of our cognition. Our collective narrative is the story of problem-solvers who have innovated, entertained and subverted our way through history.

LeDerick Horne, poet, speaker and disability rights advocate (USA).

Dyslexia and Me

Marcia Brissett-Bailey

Growing up with dyslexia hasn't been easy. For much of my life it's been traumatic, bringing down my confidence and self-esteem. It's so important to gain a greater understanding of black perspectives; I know from my own experience as a black woman, I have felt invisible while still appearing to be visible in a day-to-day life that does not always see me. My lived experience and struggles are invisible, as I show up in the world; this includes the way I speak, dress, my identity and my culture.

Race, gender, class, values, influences, role models and

opportunities shape us as individuals within the black community, and damage can be done if we're not supported and acknowledged by society. However, in order to achieve our goals, we can obtain professional help and guidance.

I want people to understand the importance of talking about dyslexia and the impact of race and culture for those of us who are neurodiverse. For far too long, the voices within stories about dyslexia that I've read have largely come from a white perspective. Many of us have felt silenced.

I cannot speak for every black dyslexic, as our experiences, class and environment will be different and have a different impact. In the same way, there is no single, agreed, clear definition of dyslexia. It's so complex due to its neurodiverse nature.

I didn't understand, as a young person, that I was exposed to inequalities from a very early age and that I was also carrying trauma from my parents, who were trying to find their way in a country where they did not feel they belonged. I also carried the inequalities of growing up in the UK, coming from a migrant background and being marginalized by the colour of my skin. I can see now that being black, a woman and in particular being dyslexic magnified my feelings of being less of a person.

As a first-generation, black British-born migrant, with parents from Jamaica, I am from a time when children were seen but not heard; we displayed respect and good manners to adults and elders, whoever they were. I am not sure if this was always a good thing but this is how it was.

My mother believed in tough love and discipline. I now know this came from her own upbringing in Jamaica – she came to England when she was eight years old. There are many moments I have captured in my memory, with Mum helping me to build my motivation and resilience as I learned to ride a bike, getting back onto my bike no matter how many times I fell, grazed my knee, or a tear fell from my eye. She'd tell me to get back on that bike until I learned to ride, and that experience taught me to never give up.

I never have and this is why I am writing this book today.

I grew up in a Caribbean household and matriarchal family structure, in which the women were the heads of the households, planners and organizers of the home; running a home was like running a business. I understood about money needing to be stretched, about saving for a rainy day and being part of clubs called 'partner' (often pronounced 'pardner'), which were a form of savings where a group of people pay an agreed sum of money on a periodic basis. This practice has been traced back to the Yoruba Credit system. Many of the women in my family would have two jobs, one of which was cleaning offices.

My dad was very much part of my upbringing and a positive role model. He was all about play and gave our family balance. We would talk in the car, as he drove and sang songs. He came to my primary school before school started in the mornings, to play football with the boys, and I would be goalkeeper. On those days, I would gain a particular popularity. The rest of the time I felt different and often lonely. Some children were unkind.

My grandmother once told me I needed to work twice as hard as everyone else. I didn't understand at the time what she meant. Sadly, she was preparing me for the inequalities of the society and world, due to the colour of my skin. I now realize that many of my black counterparts were also told this by their parents at some point in their lives and that being dyslexic made this truer still. Such values borne from my Jamaican heritage, as many Caribbean households will know, have enriched me in navigating a system with so many systematic barriers.

Growing up in the 1980s, on a council housing estate in Hackney, East London, gave me a particular experience in life. Growing up in the 'flats' was like growing up with one big family and everyone looked out for each other's children. Adults who knew us, and sometimes those who didn't, would tell us off like an uncle or auntie if they saw us doing anything wrong. I recall those days when your door was always open to your neighbour and you could knock for a chat or if you ran out of sugar or milk.

In all of my times of trauma, of not being able to read or spell, of having problems with short-term memory and having to learn visually over and over again to remember, I've come to realize that my upbringing and life experiences growing up in the flats taught me resilience. This was an advantage in preparing me for adulthood. I learned the importance of play, creativity, friendship and community. Living in the flats there were differences but it was never about the colour of your skin. We were all from different backgrounds: Scottish, Caribbean, Maltese, Turkish, African, Irish, white British, mixed family; many elderly ladies were from Jewish heritage. I never felt prepared for the inequalities of society in the outside world...

I recall as a child being very accident-prone, breaking glasses, somehow knocking my foot on the side of a door or chair leg, far too often. My grandma realized this, I could sense it, and I knew it myself too but I didn't understand why this was happening, as I so much wanted to please and help my grandma in the kitchen and make her feel proud.

Primary school was meant to be a nurturing foundation of learning but it's the place that gave me many traumatic scars. I developed a deep anxiety that started between fourth and fifth year (Years 5 and 6 in today's terms/US Grades 4 and 5, aged 9–11), before transitioning to secondary school. I felt I had to learn to survive in education, staying afloat mentally and physically, so I would not sink. It was when we had to read aloud, with the teacher letting each table around the class take turns, that I developed my stammer, which remained right through into secondary school. The label 'stutterer' was left ringing in my ears from those around me. I would blank out and want the ground to swallow me up.

I felt frustrated, ashamed and different. All I wanted was to be the same as my peers. This left the biggest impact on my learning, as well as leaving me struggling with fear, sweaty hands and heart palpitations. It was a whole-body experience that made me sick to my core. On top of that, maths and its rules were a total puzzle to me.

I made the decision to write with such small letters, you almost needed a magnifying glass to see. I thought this would mean my teachers wouldn't be able to read my spelling mistakes. It would take me so long to complete any written work, I sometimes had to stay in class at playtime (recess) to finish. It was hard seeing my friends outside, while I struggled to write clearly. Forming each letter needed so much effort and concentration. My handwriting today is still not consistent and I have written things that I cannot read back. I can now accept and live with having untidy handwriting as it's just part of me.

My mum and dad wanted a better life for me than they had had (in the days of signs saying 'no dogs, no Irish, no blacks'). However, my Mum could see there was a delay in my learning compared with other children in the family and she went to my primary school demanding that I receive help. I now know she saw herself in me and she didn't want me to struggle as she had.

By this time, I already felt different from my peers and became selectively mute. I was doing everything I could to be invisible in class. I felt frustrated and stupid. If ever I spoke and asked for help, I was told to use a dictionary, but if I could not spell a word, how could I look it up? This left me lost, although ironically, the dictionary became my best friend. I ended up reading it like a regular book, memorizing words and placing them into my memory bank. I would overthink everything I was writing; my brain would go at 150 miles per hour and needed a personal assistant to organize all the files, which held all my memories and ideas. I could sense there was a low expectation from my teachers and the school. They didn't have to say anything, I could feel it; I could tell how differently they would engage with the others around me.

While writing this book, my dad gave me my primary school reports to read. I read a report dated 2 June 1984. It stated, 'Marcia has tried hard in all areas of the curriculum, she has made some progress in reading but lacks confidence with unfamiliar texts even when they are within her capabilities. Marcia has made every effort to improve her written work. She still requires help to organize and express her ideas, in written form and needs a lot of assistance with spelling.' It then goes on to say, 'Marcia finds mathematics difficult but is making slow progress with a lot of practical activity reinforcing concepts.'

This report was written when I was 10 years, 11 months and 2 days old, forming my end of year report before going to secondary school. This was also the time when my class teacher told my parents that I wasn't going to achieve academically.

Although I feel the report highlighted I was clearly struggling at school, it did not mention any of my strengths; it was all about how well I behaved and my difficulties with learning in a linear way. I remember this made me feel that I didn't belong. I was so traumatized by the whole experience. Somehow I still loved school and wanted to learn, but school did not love me back.

I knew I was not stupid. I simply struggled with the written word and this has always made me wonder, did my working-class background, race, environment or gender limit my opportunities and result in my not being diagnosed with dyslexia?

I had the mindset to learn, and the influences of my cultural background helped me to stay focused on my goals, as failure was not an option; there was always feedback that I could learn and move forward from.

At secondary school, sport was a lifesaver, showing me I could excel and helping me to develop teamwork, communication and leadership skills. I found more ways to mask my difficulties in learning, spending long hours completing homework, though feeling a great deal of self-doubt and negativity.

I made myself emotionally absent and would daydream for hours if I didn't understand what the teachers were saying. I believed I couldn't keep asking the teacher for help, as the class was just going too fast. I did have a weekly session with a support teacher. I wrote stories with her and learned that I had a good imagination and was able to build ideas, and create and visualize stories.

When I sat for my final GCSE exams, I remember a paper being placed in front of me. Truly, I didn't have a clue what it said. Everything went blank. It was like a foreign language and it felt as if I had been set up to fail. After all those years studying, I achieved one GCSE with a grade B in drama. Even at that age, I felt the school had failed me, a working-class girl who they didn't try to get to know to find out how my mind might work.

At college, my dyslexia was diagnosed. I was 16 and couldn't have been more relieved. I was no longer 'stupid'. There was a name for the way I learned and saw the world in pictures. My parents didn't really understand my diagnosis, nor did they know about dyslexia, but I received weekly support from a lady called Jenny, to whom I will be forever grateful.

I felt released from a prison sentence but I was innocent of the crime, left dealing with crippling emotions. I felt savagely deprived of the opportunity to know who I was and the true potential I carried inside me. I'd been held back and all I wanted to do was learn to read but I had inside me my mother's mantra: to never give up.

You can see in Chapter 3 how Ayana, my daughter, received an earlier diagnosis, had a much more successful time at school, though she also had many struggles as a person with dyslexia.

College was the best thing that happened to me. I learned about myself. I was listened to. My views and voice were heard and I was given the tools to develop strategies to support the way I learned, and I ran with it. The jigsaw pieces of my life started fitting together.

I was failed at both primary and secondary school by a system that wasn't created with me in mind. Even at college, the structure of the education system and its inequalities ran deep and brought great difficulties, but I still wanted to learn and had goals and dreams to achieve academically. I had to work exceptionally hard to jump over hurdles and through hoops. There was definitely discrimination about my colour and my social class, and I came to realize that it wasn't me that was broken but the system.

In later years, my mum told me it was suggested to her that my problems with learning were linked to problems at home, possibly abuse. When I think about that now, my blood boils. It feels to me that racist assumptions were being made, stereotypes of a working-class black family. I had chosen not to speak but this was linked to my learning, and wanting to feel invisible, hiding from the nightmare of feeling different, escaping from the way my mind went blank when I tried to write. They wanted to blame my parents.

It was also at college that I became aware that while things were going positively, I didn't know any other dyslexic people who looked like me, or anyone from a cultural background other than white people who were dyslexic. This made me feel isolated when reaching out to the dyslexic community. I felt as if I was the only one. Dyslexia seemed to be a middle-class experience, hence the need for this book.

I am the first member of my family to go to university and gain a degree. Since then, I have gained a postgraduate degree in career guidance and a master's degree in special educational needs and disabilities. I still have conflicting voices in my head from my childhood. I still have to work twice as hard as my peers. I know now that dyslexia is not an indicator of intelligence, but being told for so long that I wasn't good enough did take its toll. I had to stop sabotaging myself and start believing in myself, from a place of self-love and acceptance.

On top of this, when I started my journey into adulthood, I started to feel that everything that represented me was portrayed as negative. There were no images of anyone who looked like me that represented beauty; people of my skin colour did not achieve academically, according to the statistics.

Only when in my mid-20s did I meet my friend Alice, who is also in this book, who is black, dyslexic and dyspraxic; someone I could relate to and did not have to explain my story to. While completing my research paper, I met Donald Schloss, who is black, dyslexic and the founder of the Adult Dyslexia Organization. Donald was so supportive in my quest for knowledge and research on dyslexia, he became a role model, as I had never met a black person who was managing an organization before, within the dyslexic space. I no longer felt alone in a society that had excluded me. I was truly inspired to continue to believe in me, my goals and aspirations.

My bubble burst when I entered the labour market, seeking full-time employment. Leaving university, I felt fearless and I was always confident about disclosing my dyslexia on an application form. On additional support I would say, 'I am dyslexic but this does not affect my ability to do the job'. I was always good at interviews, as I could talk for England. Tests were harder but I would try my best and ask for extra time. It can be extremely frustrating being the one to ask for help during an interview process, when you have already disclosed facts about yourself, and even the employers were not always inclusive to someone like me. Not always having reasonable adjustments can make one anxious and isolated, resonant to how I often felt at school.

From my experience, Human Resources (HR) in organizations still have some work to do around disability and being inclusive and not just treating it like a 'tick-box' exercise. Equality, equity and inclusion need to be embedded into organizational culture, via leadership, management and staff training, in order to promote neurodiversity in the workplace.

I try to focus on my talents and strengths, as I have a tendency to foresee the end of the project before the beginning. I then realize no one is with me and I have to work my way backwards. I've learned to view seeing the end goal first as a strength. I did feel in some employment, it was like being back at school again. I have seen staff who are dyslexic, including myself, shed a few tears, feeling bullied and misunderstood, developing anxiety and also staying late at work to complete tasks.

I am learning to understand about the glass ceiling, which represents an invisible barrier that prevents people from progressing to senior levels in an organizational hierarchy, owing to (for example) their class or race. I was already fighting the system with dyslexia, which was an invisible disability. I was reluctant to apply for any leadership roles as my white counterparts did, even though I may have had more qualifications, including a degree and experience at the time. I often saw the struggle of many of my black colleagues new to these roles, trying to get their voices heard.

The portrayal of a black woman, via labels in society, can really be hard. Black women can be depicted as angry and aggressive, wrapped up in institutional (also known as systemic) racism, which is embedded as normal practice within society and organizations. I realize now that that is not the type of woman who raised and nurtured me. I am not aggressive. I would say I have had to be assertive to get my voice heard.

There were many times in the workplace when I had to tell myself every day I was good enough, and I guess my passion comes from that, wanting to empower others to find their voice, rise above adversity and be their true, authentic selves. Not every organization is going to be for me, especially if their culture and diversity make me feel as if I do not belong, where I am visible but still feel invisible.

When I am in a non-inclusive environment, aspects of myself become the subject or topic of conversation: my hair, my dress of African print, 'Are you religious? Do you wear a headscarf for religious purposes? Your accent sounds like East London. I may be dyslexic as well, as I cannot spell. How long have you been dyslexic? What country were you born in?' Even if I respond with, 'I was born in London', this is usually followed up with, 'Okay, where were your parents born – in Africa or the Caribbean?'

There is a real conversation about intersectionality and identity to be had when you experience this sort of questioning on a daily basis.

I am unapologetically a black woman...

I am unapologetically dyslexic...

I am unapologetically ME!

There are so many layers in my lived experience of being dyslexic, a woman and black. I have only given you a snippet, as have those who have shared their stories in this book. There are so many untold stories that need to be told when talking about dyslexia from a cultural perspective and the social factors that have had an impact in shaping people's lives.

I have shared my journey with dyslexia from primary and secondary school to college and the workplace; I will leave motherhood and dyslexia, for now. I feel that this needs a book all to itself on raising a child with dyslexia, navigating the education system and managing home life.

As a result of my personal experiences, I am keen to raise awareness within black communities, to break the silence and tackle the stigma surrounding dyslexia. I am also keen to empower others with dyslexia, to enable them to have a voice and share their lived experience from a cultural perspective, to reflect the dyslexic community. We are not broken, but the education system is broken and outdated; it is no longer fit for purpose. Rote learning and memory testing are clearly not enough.

I have come to embrace my dyslexia as being part of me but not defining me. Dyslexia has challenges but I would not change who I am. My main issue is that my learning difference was not identified at school, so I lacked support to build on my strengths and explore the advantages of dyslexia.

I have learned to build on my strengths and am grateful for those who saw my potential. I built resilience and changed my mindset from 'can't' to 'can' and came to unlearn the negative thoughts.

I am now unapologetic and not ashamed to say I am dyslexic.

Bringing my own folding chair to the table enables me to get my voice heard at the table and share it all. This enables me to be free and be me.

———

Marcia Brissett-Bailey, listed as one of Women Beyond the Box's Top 50 Influential Neurodivergent Women 2022, British Dyslexia Association BDA Adult Award 2022 sponsored by Texthelp, author, narrative changer, Forbes featured, Co-founder of the British Dyslexia Association's Cultural Perspective Committee, BDA Observer of the Executive Board, Waltham Forest Dyslexia Association trustee, Advisory Board Member of Centre for Neurodiversity at Work and Co-production Board Member of Neurodiversity in Business.

> Letters swapped in silence
> Spelling dad instead of bad
> Stutters feeling timeless
> In the little space we had
> We move, we shift, adjust and lift
> So nobody can see
> But when doors close our eyes grow cold from straining just
>   to read
> Wipe your tears and lift your crown
> There's little time to mope and frown
> Forgotten passwords bring you down but they won't kill you
> Sticks and stones may break my bones but poor
>   performance haunts me
> The eldest born, a migrant home, the language gap had
>   caught me
> No words for SpLD, neurodiversity or access needs
> But over time I've come to love the different parts of me
> Black, dyslexic, out the box, young, wild and free
> I swap my letters, loud and proud and I don't care who sees.

Vivienne Isebor, Founder and Managing Director of ADHD Babes, Clinical Associate in Psychology of East London NHS Foundation Trust, and performing artist.

Dyslexia to PhD

William Carter

I went to a school in a leafy, white, middle-class area, which was very unequal in a sense that you had both rich and poor living on the same street. Some people thought that this was good for me. I did not quite think so because I found that I became quite alienated and isolated, being in a school with rich kids. You see, there were kids who had nannies dropping them off to school every day in Range Rovers and Mercedes; they had people who were paid to look after them. Often, these same families would go to America or Paris for the weekend. From an early age, I began to realize the contours of class, and in particular, how class relates to race. I also noticed that mostly every mixed-race kid tended to have a white mother, and black dad who wasn't in the picture; also, that they were poor and lived in a council house, and that I was one of them.

I remember when in school, if the white kids did anything wrong, they would be classed as cheeky, or rebellious, whereas, if I misbehaved, teachers would use the word 'criminal' when addressing me. Teachers would say things like, 'You don't want to be a criminal when you grow up' or, 'Start acting your actual age.'

I found primary school hard and I could not keep up with the other kids. They were learning the alphabet and times tables and I could not do that. When I got to Reception and Year 1 (US Preschool and Kindergarten, aged five to six), this was where I was 'forced' to learn that I was stupid. This was the time when we were put into sets and the way I remember it is the higher the set you were (and sets were from 1 to 5), the closer you were to the teacher. Because I could not keep up, I was given bits of paper to cut up and stick onto other pieces of paper, while others were being taught how to read and do their times tables. Things were so hard that eventually I was put on a table by myself.

I found reading difficult, and speaking in front of people was always a horrible experience. Every time I was told to read and I would not know how to say a word, I was immediately vilified and made fun of. To make matters worse, there was the Handwriting Licence. Basically, once your handwriting was extremely neat, you received a licence and rather than continue writing in pencil, you could now write in pen. I used a pencil throughout my time in primary school.

Even my mum was 'left out' many times, if not all the time. You see, if you had all the rich kids mixing together, then all their parents would too. This meant my mum would never be included and often would feel left out. It often felt as if my role in school was to just sit back and let the rich kids become the doctors and lawyers, as I never received any support. I felt, as a mixed-raced boy, that I was a stain on the school. In other words, as if I was already a criminal.

Secondary school was a different experience. It was much more diverse than primary school and a lot more inclusive. There were people from all different backgrounds, and I felt that the teachers treated me as if I belonged in the school, rather than as an outsider. So, things improved for me socially but became ever more challenging for me academically. I found it hard to write things down and preferred to type. However, when I asked if I could get some funding for a laptop, I was told no, because I was doing 'well enough' so the school could not justify paying for a computer. It was not until I was about 12 or 13 years old that I started getting help. After a long, hard battle, I eventually received funding. I just felt I had to go through a lot, unnecessarily, to get the help I rightfully deserved.

When it came for me to apply for A-levels, teachers often tried to put me off, saying that I would not be able to keep up and maybe I should study at a technical college. After some encouragement from a genuinely nice teacher, I applied to study politics, geography and psychology. So, we got to results day and I turned up at school 7am and saw one of the teachers staring at me but not directly at my eyes. She almost looked embarrassed. You see, my teachers could not believe what score I achieved, as I was not good enough for A-levels. I ended up getting 100 per cent in politics and 99 per cent in psychology, the highest scores in the school ever, and also in the country. When word got round the school of my grades, no one could believe it. I was even told, 'Oh that is the white side that got you those grades.' I was in a place now where I wanted teachers to feel ashamed of how they had treated me and how they had made me feel.

All these experiences have made me want to make a change and disprove the notion that a black, working-class, dyslexic kid cannot do what they want to do in life. I don't want to be the exception to the rule, I want to be proof that rules can be broken.

However, I still could not get into Cambridge University, being told that there were other students who had significantly superior academic records compared with me. It really upset my frequency, or should I say, my path. I was not meant to get good grades; I should have been in prison by now, as I was deemed a criminal in primary school. By the time I applied and went to university, there were various assisted learning tools that I could access. These aids would read out books to me, which was great, as I cannot handle reading straight from a book. There were audio books and text-to-speech apps that helped a great deal. I was accepted to my second choice, Bristol University, and was fortunate to get a Fulbright Scholarship to study for my master's and PhD in America.

I spent ages on my personal statement for the Fulbright Scholarship, to study at Berkeley University, in California. Then I attended an interview, which included the Chancellor of Cardiff University, Chancellor of Liverpool University, the Head of Medicine at Cambridge, Head of Medicine at Oxford and the Head of the Fulbright Commission. It was a very intense interview, at times somewhat intimidating. After this, I received an email that I had been accepted on a Fulbright Scholarship. In addition, I was nominated for the Opportunity Award and for the Alumni Award, the top Fulbright Scholarship in the world.

I thought back to when I was younger, being told I was stupid. I thought, 'Right, I am going to bring light to these barriers. I want to talk about all the limitations that one must overcome.'

I now live in California and will be here for the next six years, doing a PhD in Black Geographies, which includes topics on The Middle Passage, race, class and sociology. The first two to three years are the master's and the remainder will be the PhD. I am keen on going into politics. When growing up you always feel that your life is dependent on the good decisions of others. However, these decision-makers do not look like me or have my experiences. So, at each stage, I want to show how illegitimate this education system is and how unfair it is; how structurally unfair it is. How structurally you have those being steered towards being a doctor or a lawyer, whereas others are structurally steered towards the life of criminality.

I feel as if I am almost making up for those classes that I could not take in primary school.

My philosophy in life is to try to ensure that others do not have to go through what I went through. I remember a quote that they always try to motivate black children with. The quote was from Malcom X: 'Education is the passport to the future, it belongs to those who prepare for it today.' I hated this quote because what if you try so hard for education and prepare and it is not accessible to you? It is not always motivation that you need – it is sometimes support and access, and we should be incredibly careful when we use the word 'motivation' and maybe use the word 'accessibility' instead.

––––

William Carter, UC Berkeley PhD student, Fulbright Scholar, Bristol Politics BSc First Class with Honours, neurodiversity campaigner and public speaker.

"Sometimes you may feel that you are on your own, but dyslexia is very common. Don't let it be an obstacle to achieving what you want in life!

Sandra Iris Wolo, Founder and CEO of Africa Dyslexics United (UK and Congo), also known as Adult Dyslexics Unit.

Primary to Secondary School

Ayana Bailey

I am 14 years of age and both my parents are of Jamaican heritage and first-generation British-born, which I guess makes me second-generation British-born.

In this chapter, I share my experience as a young girl with dyslexia. So far, I do not see my dyslexia stopping me from doing what I want, as the older I get, I have a better understanding of my strengths and know where I can get the right support.

While in Year 5 (US Grade 4, aged nine), I had my first dyslexia screening, at the Waltham Forest Dyslexia Association (WFDA).

This included attending tutoring classes once a week, with two dyslexia teachers, for support with maths and English.

The tutors provided me with strategies and techniques that I did not receive at school, which included creating revision cards for specific spelling of words that I used every day. I also played spelling games on my tutor's iPad, which really built my confidence. I felt listened to and understood by both my tutors, Maxine and Carol.

Attending the tutoring class at WFDA allowed me the time to build my confidence and to think and process the information, as there were only two students in the class. My voice could finally be heard and questions could be answered, to gain a better understanding of my lessons.

I cannot stress enough how important it has been to find and use my voice.

I have spoken in front of 200 people, talking about my business, Yani Creations, which I developed in Year 6 (US Grade 5), becoming a CEO at the age of ten, based on my passion to inspire young people to build their confidence through positive quotes and affirmations.

Primary school years

My mum, with support from my dad, pushed for my primary school to provide an educational psychologist assessment for a diagnosis. All along, my school did not identify a need for an assessment, as my parents were told by the school that I was on par with my peers. I was always strong at English but really struggled in maths and would sometimes be tearful during class.

I remember doing the assessment over two days, after which I was diagnosed with dyslexia. This enabled me to get extra support during Year 6 for the standard assessment tests (SATs). A tutor would take me out of the class, to help me with spelling, punctuation and grammar (SPAG). I also received some support for maths.

At primary school, some of my challenges were with SPAG, in particular grammar. For example, I especially had difficulties knowing where I should put commas. However, at the time, I did not feel any different from my friends.

My Year 6 class teacher, Mr P (Deputy Head of Year), was amazing and supportive and he truly helped me because he understood exactly the things I had difficulty with and had an exceptional understanding of dyslexia.

Secondary school years, where I am currently

In secondary school, I am starting to understand the importance of finding my voice, especially as I enter Year 10 (US Grade 9) and start my GCSEs. My mum has really supported me, by sharing her own experience at secondary school (as she is also dyslexic), and has helped me to find strategies to focus on my strengths. So, my dyslexia doesn't feel as if it's a struggle but part of what makes me, me.

My mum has also taught me about being creative in my thinking and using visuals in my learning, especially when revising for exams. It can be frustrating sometimes at school, as I feel forced to learn in a way that does not feel natural to me, especially when I know my way of thinking cannot fit into a box.

However, sometimes I find it really hard to speak up, especially in my maths lessons, where I just cannot keep up with the class. It takes me so long to process what is being said that I sometimes come away from the class not learning much. This has made me feel sad and as if I do not fit in, even though I really want to learn. Not feeling confident in maths has left me not wanting to keep asking questions, as I feel I would be slowing the class down.

These issues, especially at the beginning of secondary school, were quite a challenge for me, and teachers seem to simply misunderstand the challenges dyslexic people can face in 'conventional' teaching environments. It would be more helpful if teachers could break down the tasks, step by step. Most of the time they just explain the task once and think you understand it first time but I don't most of the time. My parents have spoken to the school special educational needs and disabilities co-ordinator (SENDCo) and my maths teachers. My parents were told that I need to put my hand up more or stay after class and ask questions. The SENDCo also suggested that I attend the Maths Club after school. This makes me feel even more nervous and I have not yet attended.

My mum often says to me, 'No one can put you down when you feel confident and believe in yourself.' I am learning to follow this advice but often I struggle with this at times as a young person. I recall a peer saying in my class after lesson, how 'I must be dyslexic' because I had difficulty reading what was on the board. I replied to him and said, 'Well, I am dyslexic' and that I could read the board. The boy didn't say anything more.

On another occasion in class, the teacher was speaking and we were supposed to write down everything she was saying in our books. I didn't know how to spell one of the words that she said, so I then asked the teacher to spell it out for me. One of the girls sitting behind me said, 'That's an easy word to spell.' I told her I was dyslexic, because I do feel comfortable telling people I am, as it's a part of who I am. The girl appeared to feel sorry for me. I told her not to feel sorry for me because dyslexia is an amazing thing to have. I must own it and not be embarrassed about my abilities.

I am very creative and love to be in my own little world. I have chosen drama and photography for my options at GCSE but I also love sociology and was sad to have to drop it. Thinking about this reminds me of an incident that is a perfect example of my dyslexia. We were learning about

Marxism in sociology and the teacher asked me, in class, to say what was explained in the lesson and tell the class what it was all about. I knew in my head what I wanted to say but just couldn't find the words and I just froze. I could have comfortably explained my thoughts in a diagram/mind-map and shown the key words of my understanding of Marxism but I was not asked to do so.

I know I struggle, like any of my peers, with some subjects, but I do need my lessons taught sometimes at a slower pace. I can also be sensitive to sounds, so I guess there are different aspects to my dyslexia for me as an individual that I am still learning about.

Extra-curricular activities

My parents have given me so much support and encouragement to try new things, like swimming, performing arts and bike riding. This has also helped me to build my confidence and find my strengths, to follow my interests and passions.

I really believe having the opportunity to try new things has led me to not just focus on my dyslexia as being negative. It made me realize that I can learn, it's just that I need to be given or find other ways to do so. My new-found confidence has led me to audition for lead roles in my school productions of *Annie*. Most recently I was Charlotte Church in *We Will Rock You*, and Edna, Tracy's mum, in *Hairspray*. Taking part in school activities has certainly helped me to find out what I am good at and enjoy.

I am still a very shy person and have times when I do not feel so confident but I think it's so important that I have tried new things. Understanding what interests me has helped me know the advantages of my dyslexia.

I believe it's really important to ask for help and I am learning that if I do not ask, I will not get the support I need. It is equally important to feel safe to ask those questions in a classroom environment.

Furthermore, having Maxine as my tutor from Year 6 to now has been so positive, seeing other people who are black like me, inspiring me to be the best I can be; she also understands my cultural background, which can be really helpful to my learning.

Alongside my parents making me aware that it is okay to ask for help, I am also realizing that everyone asks for help in different ways. Being dyslexic allows me to see and think a little differently and I feel that different thinkers are important too.

As young as I am, I live by my business motto: 'Be *you*, be unique.'

———

Ayana Bailey, CEO and Founder of Yani Creations, creative creator, actor and entrepreneur.

The positive aspects of dyslexia

Working with dyslexic students has taught me that being dyslexic has many advantages. One advantage that many dyslexic people have is the ability to think outside the box; this enables them to have brilliant and innovative ideas. Furthermore, due to their excellent logical reasoning and visual abilities they are likely to pursue rewarding careers in the mathematical or science fields. It saddens me when someone unwittingly believes that if you have dyslexia, you lack intelligence. This assumption is so far from the truth.

Maxine Johnson, freelance dyslexia specialist teacher, BEd (Hons) PG Dip SpLD (Dyslexia), APC, AMBDA, MDG, PATOSS (UK).

The Common Difference

4

Remi Ray

My name is Remi Ray and I am a Black British woman of Caribbean heritage; my parents were born here in the UK but all of my grandparents were born in Jamaica. This background culture enabled me to enter the world with tough skin. I grew up with a brother, two sisters, loads of cousins and family friends, who often gathered with their children at my auntie's house at the top of Peckham, in London, and so I always had groups of relatable people to bond with. Before gentrification became so vast in Peckham, it was easy to see others who looked just like my family members or me, and there was always a sense of freedom that shot through me each and every time I hit the high street as a child with my mum. This is significant in my journey to entrepreneurship because this was my first understanding of community.

My grandmother would walk these streets too and connect with others who had travelled to the UK looking for work. Growing up in a place like Peckham, which had very little opportunity, was also my first module in life's business school of resilience, community and action. Walking the streets, you had to have your wits about you, as there was a lot of gang violence and frequent fatalities; the community would often step in to calm things down and there was always common respect for families.

These tragedies kept me on my toes, helped me build integrity and gave me the drive to 'want-to-want' better for myself. I attended the local primary school and had many friends throughout the school years. I was not too fond of school but always enjoyed the engagement with my peers. I spent years shying away from any advancement in academia and could always be found being disruptive, getting my classmates together to be creative for a common cause or for sport. As I child, I was decorated for my efforts in netball, volleyball and even rugby; I excelled as a team player and would often be in the local newspapers. I doubled my efforts in those areas because of my efforts in class always being below par. I struggled so much in school, I lost the confidence to apply myself and I left secondary school with barely any grades. I worked triple-hard at college to get back on track and spent the next three years repairing and strategizing the best route to get into university to study fashion.

I took an Access to Fashion Business course at the London College of Fashion, and that's where I first learned the word 'dyslexia'. I was tested towards the end of my first year in university and was diagnosed as dyslexic. I was supported through university and graduated with a BA Hons in Fashion Management and Marketing in 2010. I left university even more confused because I was afraid of being judged in jobs because of my dyslexia, so I decided to take the route of public relations (PR) and had some of my worst experiences. I tried my hand at styling but couldn't pronounce some of the less-common brands and was once shouted at by a top stylist. I found white women in particular to not be very nurturing, and the opportunities for black people were limited. So, I decided it was time to create my own path; I took part-time jobs, including working on a market stall, and started to research how to build my own boutique. Trapped in A Skinny World was birthed in 2011, as a plus-sized vintage boutique. While the journey in entrepreneurship has been tough, with the various layers I know, it has really helped me to support others who also want to take similar paths. I was recognized in 2019 as one of the most influential neurodivergent women in the UK, for my contribution to the plus-size fashion world. I received sponsorship from all around the world, with major brands such as Simply Be. Working with many mainstream artists has shone a light on the plus-size industry.

I now run The Diverse Creative Community Interest Company

(CIC), as a support hub for other dyslexic people. This achievement is by far my favourite, because, through the tears of education, I am proof that as dyslexic people go, we can find a way.

My superpower is the ability to see opportunities before others do. It may sound a little egotistical but I am my biggest champion. Reflecting on a lot of the work I have done, not many people were able to see the vision before I took action and gave myself pep talks to begin. I now use my voice to help those who may have been struggling alone for a long time to see the light at the end of the tunnel. I guess that makes me relatable. As a neurodiversity mindset coach, I am able to see opportunities and simplify things for others. I coach, as this stands for everything that I wish had been done for me.

The biggest challenges with dyslexia were the lack of support in jobs, the lack of consideration from senior leadership in roles and the lack of care for those who are different. It has been crucial to seek support, even If I have had to pay for it, and to use software to help me to prepare.

I now realize that all this time, what I was searching for was Remi, so I am passionate about returning to self. Personal development requires no friends; it is about finding self-advocacy and reminding yourself who you are and knowing that your 'home' is 'you'.

I am the founder of the Shit Happens Fund for the community, intended to help women with finances and give women a voice and the confidence that they can do things, such as save money.

I don't believe that everything has to derive from pain. We need a new narrative and to stop carrying around the trauma.

I am one of four children; my mum brought us up by herself and my dad is an addict. I was an anomaly in my family strand. Most of my friends had kids really young. However, my path has been different. People should see us as lighthouses!

——

Remi Ray, neurodivergent high-performance coach, one of Women Beyond the Box's Top 50 Influential Neurodivergent Women 2019, entrepreneur, creative business strategist, Programme Curator and Founder of The Diverse Creative CIC.

> I don't fit into this world; you put me under too much pressure as a young Black Man.

Chesney Ellis-Browne Instagram: @the_gymbully

Dyslexic and Thriving

Oladoyin Idowu

I have thought long and hard for the best phrase to explain how I felt for so many years, living with dyslexia and not knowing what it was. It was a constant feeling of being betrayed by the people you love and expect to protect you. Even though I have come to

understand that they were trying to help and motivate me in their own way, their attempts at help did more damage than good.

I still have many vivid memories from secondary school in Nigeria, and how my parents made sure I had no free time to do anything else but study. My calendar was basically wake up, attend general classes, private tutoring, reading time and sleep, then repeat. Their response to my complaints on how I was struggling with school was more teachers and reinforcements. The more resources used to help me learn, the greater the frustration when it was not yielding any results – and rest assured that they took it out on me.

Some of my teachers even attempted motivation by calling out everybody's test scores to the entire class, which was always humiliating for me, as I always had the low scores and they proceeded to flog me for it.

I do not think anything else can illustrate 'rock bottom' better than the day my dad was so angry with me that he asked me to get a notepad and pen to calculate how much money he had wasted on me that year.

Item number 1 was my school fees, and yes it was a waste because there was no result to show for it. Today I still have a vivid memory of kneeling down there, wailing, holding the pen and shaking. To do that exercise was the hardest and most painful thing I have ever had to do in my life, and worse yet was being asked to do it by my ever-loving and most supportive father. I remember when I finished that exercise and was released to go to my room, the tears did not stop flowing till I slept, tired and frail from crying so much.

My undiagnosed dyslexia made me feel invisible, helpless, clueless – you name it. It was as if I was locked up in a tight box, with no ventilation and no keys to open it up.

I eventually got to the point where I felt I had no real reason to live. My future was bleak. The only pathway I knew to success involved good academic achievements and it was clear how that was going. I knew for a fact that modelling wasn't for me either. I convinced myself I had no future and was ready to take all the drugs I could find at home, but a friend stopped me before I could go any further. I was angry with her for a long time but now I could not be more grateful for the timing of her intervention.

I was still convinced that there was something wrong inside me. What other explanation could there possibly be as to why I couldn't read and acquire knowledge, no matter how much time I spent trying to? I decided to find another way, so I told my parents I was done with school. I am sure you can paint a picture in your head as to their reaction to this and you would mostly be accurate. Undaunted, I stood my ground. I was really done, feeling empty and worthless. I had to think, 'What next, where do I go from here?'

It was a very big question that would determine the course of my life.

I opted to learn culinary skills, then proceeded to learn about decoration for events, then about set design... Yes, as you have guessed, once I discovered something I could do well, I couldn't stop. My parents happily paid for it, and even though I struggled with some aspects of it, they could finally see results.

Fast forward to the day I wanted answers as to why I was dumb. I typed into Google the one-million-dollar question, 'Am I dumb?' So many things came up in the search but one thing caught my eye. There was an article about learning disorders and why students may feel they are dumb. I do not remember all the details of this article. I remember it being lengthy and there was too much to read but despite the fact that I considered reading to be laborious, it was explaining things I could relate to. When I came across the word 'dyslexia' and what it meant, I am sure I felt exactly how Archimedes felt when he said the word, 'EUREKA!'

It really was my eureka moment. Finally, I had an identity. It made sense, and it was great to drop the weight of all the many years of self-blaming. I did not fully understand the implication of what it meant to be dyslexic at the time and it honestly did not matter. All that mattered in that moment was that I was something; it had a name and I was not all the many other things I had been called in the past. Of course, I cried.

I used an online test which confirmed I was dyslexic but I was determined to get a physical test done, as I needed hard evidence to prove this to my parents, so it wasn't considered an attempt at making excuses for being lazy. I looked around for centres, I searched the internet; I could not find any centre in Nigeria. I asked people around me but it was an unknown word and they had no idea where I could go for a test. I settled with the online test result I had, then came the time to speak to my parents about it.

I approached them by first having them read up on the word
'dyslexia' and I came back later, enthusiastic to know what
they had discovered, only to find that they had not engaged
with the process. Oh, I was pained, but I was still determined
to tell them about it. So I created a dyslexia website, had
my dad read it and proceeded to tell them that I had the
condition.

My mum, being very religious, rebuked every spirit of learning
disability in me; my dad on the other hand reluctantly agreed;
he said, 'Well, yes, you share similar characteristics to what
is listed here but I would not want you to see yourself in the
light of having a limitation or disorder.' He concluded that
I could apply the strategies to help myself but I shouldn't
use the label. They both lived in denial again, in their bid to
protect me from society seeing me as disabled.

I honestly do not consider dyslexia to be a disability but that
is not the focus for now. My parents' reaction to this was
interesting because my mum is actually a teacher and not
once had she come across the term 'dyslexia' in any of the
numerous teacher trainings she had attended. I proceeded
to ask other teachers and the responses were similar. It was
clear that there was a gap. In Nigeria, we would spend more
time engaging in rituals, such as binding and casting demons,
than attending to an issue that had a solution. If only we paid
a little more attention to understanding what the issue was.
It was clear that we couldn't see past people's conditions or
impairments and we needed to understand that people are a
lot more than the challenges they have. I decided to immerse

myself in more research on dyslexia. I needed to help myself and learn how to navigate this identity, and there was also a need to address all the negative emotions I had developed over time. There were so many people to forgive, there was so much pain to resolve and it was evident I also needed therapy. This was how the field of psychology also came onto my radar.

Determined to get my life back in order, I embarked on the journey of living with my dyslexia, as well as the other psychological conditions I may have. Most of it was self-help, as it was majorly unknown and unexplored in Nigeria, but I did get guidance from some people. I remember my aunt, Dr Adetoun Adeola, helping me search for organizations that could help within her network, as she was a medical doctor for a non-governmental organization here in Nigeria. I remember speaking to a few other people and there was a clear gap in the knowledge about dyslexia, as well as how to access psychological therapy. It was always either non-existent or not affordable.

So, I took it upon myself to speak out. At first, this was from a place of anger. I was angry about all I had had to endure; in my opinion, the cost of ignorance was too high, it had almost cost me my life and future. I wondered how many more like me there were, so I knew for a fact that I couldn't stop until something was done about it. That was the beginning of my journey as a dyslexia advocate. I reached out to organizations like Noticeability and Billy's Quest, in the United States. I now had an entire community, and a supportive one at that, though there were a million and one constraints due to the distance and issues with accessing good technology on my part. The support was great still. I wouldn't stop talking about dyslexia. The conversations I was having on dyslexia in Nigeria eventually birthed the One Word Africa Foundation (OWAF) in October 2016, with the tagline: 'One Word at a time till everyone can learn.' OWAF is an organization whose mission is to ensure that everyone living with dyslexia can access quality education. Working on OWAF was the key I needed to unlock the box I was trapped in. The fulfilment I got from meeting and working with people with dyslexia was second to none, though not without its limitations, as dyslexia is still widely thought to be spiritual, or an attempt at being lazy. The bureaucracy to get the government to have teachers trained and develop policies for people living with dyslexia to access school accommodations is frustrating, but if there is anything my past has gifted me with, it's resilience – I won't back down.

I also started working with the skills I had acquired in set design to help me earn to do the work at One Word Africa. I got my physical dyslexia test done and my parents now support the work that I do on dyslexia. Living has become purposeful. I finally know who I am. All of this boosted my confidence to give school another attempt.

As I write this, I am typing from my bed in school, in the final year of a four-year course in psychology with a Cumulative Grade Point Average (CGPA) I could never have dreamed of. I am still determined to graduate with a higher CGPA.

My father has noted that I currently have the highest CGPA in our nuclear family, higher than his even.

Do not get me wrong, I still insist that educational achievement is not proof of a person's intelligence and worth. I am only pushing myself this hard to graduate with a perfect CGPA and proceed to do a master's degree in psychology, to encourage my tribe, The Dyslexia Tribe, and show that it can be done. Do not believe what the education system has said about you, or the many other negative ideas you have about yourself. If you have a dream, if a path does not currently exist, it is because you were engineered to create it.

My dyslexia still impacts every aspect of my life. I depend greatly on assistive technology and the multisensory learning approach. I am still navigating through life and dyslexia and everything that I am today is not despite my dyslexia but because of it. It is my sincere desire that no dyslexic person ever has to walk through this journey lonely and clueless, like I did. And I have made it my personal life mission to make it so.

———

Oladoyin Idowu, Founder of One Word Africa.

"Always remember that we are all CONNECTED!

When would now be a good idea to trust your highest thought, your clearest words and your grandest feeling? Your highest thought is always the thought which makes you feel good. Your clearest words are the words which contain truth and honesty. Your grandest feeling is LOVE.

Sabrina Ben Salmi, BSc, Mother of the Year Award Winner, author, ranked No.2 in the Pauline Long Show's 50 Most Inspirational Black Women in UK 2019.

If At First You Don't Succeed, Dust Yourself Off and Try Again

Leslie Lewis-Walker

I'm a senior 'people lead' working for the Civil Service and am of Gambian/Sierra Leone in heritage.

In most black communities in the western world, it is drilled into us that we must work twice as hard because we are black. At the same time, neurodiversity is sometimes seen as a myth, to the point where we shy away from it, as such topics are rarely discussed.

In modern-day Britain, being black comes with its challenges. For me, the lack of black people in senior leadership across all sectors illustrates that. Yes, I had to work twice as hard to gain the position I want in my life, with an added layer of having a learning disability bringing resistance in allowing me to succeed.

Growing up at home as an African and going to school or work as a British person creates a number of conflicts. At home, we listen and are taught not to rebel and not to challenge authority, but at work or school, we are taught to challenge and ask questions.

I guess I feel I have to be two different kinds of people in order to adapt but I struggle more at work because my nature of challenging is not what I grew up doing. This conflict can manifest itself in a number of ways and, for me, it's best labelled as 'imposter syndrome'. Being in a number of environments where I am the only person of colour in the room is one layer because you can't mirror yourself anywhere. Then imagine, every time I meet new people or stakeholders, I automatically go into a default mode of thinking, 'Am I going to be as "brainy" or as "intelligent" as the counterparts I will be speaking to?'

Before I feel confident in front of someone, before being too vocal, I sometimes analyse if I can hold my own in an intellectual duel. As time goes on, I am getting better at adapting and this has also made me well balanced, as listening is a key skill that not everyone has. At the same time, I have learned that all voices must be heard, as every voice is valid. I have also learned that making mistakes and not knowing is okay, in order for me to be the best version of myself and to learn about my strengths.

As a youngster, I couldn't speak until I was four years old. My mother would take me to a speech therapist on a weekly basis to help me to develop my language, as it was pretty worrying for her at the time. At primary school, I was sent to a 'special class', surrounded by young people of all disabilities, some of them extreme, with the common goal of learning how to read. At the age of ten years, I had a reading ability of a five-year-old. I was diagnosed as dyslexic when I was aged seven years. Witnessing peers excelling and learning things I had no concept of made me feel pretty isolated and my self-esteem plummeted. I was left with a low opinion of myself. On top of that, I had an extra pressure outside school, as my mother passed away when I was just ten years old.

How did I cope, you may ask? Well, I guess everything seemed to happen so fast and I tried to avoid reflecting on it all.

Secondary school was never for me either, and receiving the most unflattering GCSE and A-level results proved that the traditional ways of education didn't suit me. My main issue is working memory. I basically fell and fall on this aspect and have learned how to work round it over time. You will always see me with a 'post-it note', or a calendar reminder on my phone.

I chose to go to university and opted to study music. This was something creative I could excel at and I managed to make a name for myself afterwards. I couldn't read music because it relied heavily on using my memory to learn the different notes, so I learned how to play by ear, which served me well.

After leaving education and getting sacked from a well-known sports retailer (don't ask!), I then joined the Civil Service as an agency administrator, on a temporary basis.

The truth was that this move was purely to fund my drinking sprees at weekends and I didn't take it very seriously. The weekends would just be my escapism and my safe space because I was such a people person. However, a random, early evening conversation with a manager led me to apply for a permanent position.

Until 2013, I had had a number of roles that suited my strengths, such as engagement management and customer-facing roles. Then, after a promotion, I was exposed to a more corporate environment, which required more of an academic skillset. I struggled and this had quite a significant impact on my mental state, as I felt I wasn't good enough. Colleagues who didn't understand dyslexia didn't understand my shortcomings workwise and would get frustrated with me, leading to me becoming frustrated with myself. This prompted me to take a career break, which took me on a path of self-discovery.

I had previous experience running a cleaning business with a good friend, for a few years, on the side of my full-time job. This time round, I took a few years out for a career break to pursue a videography and marketing business, which led to me working with a variety of stakeholders, including the Metropolitan Police, MIND charity, Crystal Palace Football Club and many more. Three years of hard work paid off and within that time, I managed to rebuild my confidence and understand that my strengths really are rare and make a positive difference to my life. I re-joined the Home Office and progressed to my current role.

I guess my superpower is being emotionally intelligent. Everything boils down to people and being a good communicator, which has helped me to succeed. Having a good network helps, as can understanding that connections can be valuable. I can also see things that some people can't. Being able to empathize, executing active listening and relating through my experiences of life make me stand out. I truly think my dyslexia helps me to be more in tune with others.

With the loss of my mum and being raised by others, I know that a number of people have made me the man I am today and I owe a lot to my two aunties, cousins and friends who helped me to turn right when it was easier to go left. If I were to reflect and speak to my younger self, my top tip would be to never give up. We hear this all the time and we see loads of motivational quotes enforcing it, but it is true. I see frustration as a test of whether you want something. If you want it, you give it your all, and mindset is the first thing you can change. Time and time again, life will test you. I have failed a lot and continue to fail a lot. Every time I fail, I learn and appreciate the growth from the experience. For example, when failing at numerous tests or going for promotions and feeling that I can't learn as quickly as my peers – which, mentally, takes me back to school – I have to reflect logically on how far I have come and remind myself that this is a marathon, not a sprint.

The most valuable lesson I have learned is to acknowledge situations but not dwell on them. Every diamond comes from the rough. I, like many, have felt the frustrations of wanting to be able to be so much more on an academic level, and this will never change. One of my previous bosses used to tell me we are who we are and everyone has a gift. It is just our job to discover and use it.

____

Leslie Lewis-Walker, Senior People Lead at the UK Home Office.

It is challenging enough as a black man living here in the UK. Having to deal with the daily pressures of adulthood, but also the pressure of having to face inequality, injustice and the ignorance of some people. Discovering that I had dyslexia made me want to keep it to myself because I thought people would tell me I was using this as an excuse in the same way that I was told I was using the colour of my skin to explain the obstacles I have encountered being a black man in education. Due to the fear of judgement, I became a mute and therefore I struggled in school and college and throughout university.

I met a black professor who said he was also dyslexic, after watching me deliver a presentation to fellow students. He had seen that I overcompensated with my oration skills over my academic writing and said, 'Craig, you have such an amazing energy and the moment you learn how to do both you will be unstoppable.' Since that day, I have felt so empowered and that's why for the most part of my life since then I have gone above and beyond to get young people who look like me to embrace their dyslexia, not hide behind it, but use their uniqueness as part of their armour to demonstrate their true greatness.

We break the cycle through showing those behind us what not to do...

Craig Pinkney, criminologist and urban youth specialist, PhD researcher and Director of Solve Online Learning Centre.

The Jumbled Jammer

Winsome Duncan

My walk with dyslexia has been a long, winding and isolated road, leading to self-discovery and self-acceptance. I had always felt on the other side of stupid, until I learned that my brain processes information in a very different way.

The Black British experience of being dyslexic is one that is underserved in my opinion. We are not afforded the same support or access to equipment that can assist and help us. Being a Black dyslexic child has negative connotations and, in my opinion, it can mean being quickly mislabelled with special educational needs or attention deficit disorder or dyspraxia or whatever other negative labels teachers, heads and scholars wish to link us with when we do not level up to our white peers, without the accurate assessment processes others may receive. Yet no one wants to talk about this and they just skirt around the subject and pretend that racism does not exist within the educational institutions. I am tired of living in a whitewashed world, where I feel like I am in intellectual bondage. Most of the time I have had to be self-taught, learning by watching YouTube videos and demonstrations and through kinaesthetic play. If you talk to me too much about a topic that I am learning, I am likely to fall asleep. I need to be active in my education and I believe that I will never stop learning.

I discovered that I was dyslexic when I was 16 years old and had failed most of my GCSEs. I applied to attend Kingsway College in King's Cross, London, and met this wonderful teacher named Alice Moon, who said to me after my preliminary test, 'I think you might be dyslexic,' and I responded, 'What do you mean?' In order for me to attend the college, I had to go through the dyslexia test, which was fairly straightforward. They asked me to spell difficult words, I listened to words and wrote them out how I thought they sounded and I also read them out loud.

When I was diagnosed with dyslexia it felt like a curse to me, although this meant that I would have an extra 25 per cent of time in all my exams; God knows, I needed it. However, I never received any further support with any equipment for a laptop, dictaphone, eye wear and wasn't given different-coloured paper or notepads to write on. Did you know that black writing on a white background is really bad for dyslexic people to read? I always use a yellow or green background when editing work. The words are so much clearer in their formation.

I do not write, I scribble, and this is due to my education being disrupted three times while I was in primary school. My parents split up and we left our primary school immediately. I had no time for closure or to say goodbye to friends; I was nine years old. I was enrolled at another school, for a short stay until we were rehoused, and I contracted meningitis there. This was quite a traumatic event and I had to take time off from school to recover. Then we moved from Highbury and I went to live the rest of my childhood in Angel, Islington. I went to a primary school there. I remember on the first day, I felt as if everyone was being mean, cold and unfriendly to me. I burst into tears, shouting and pointing out, 'You don't like me, you don't like me, you don't like me.' It was just tough being in another school. It interrupted my learning and although there was some writing practice at the school, by that time my scribbles took over. I would always be jealous of those who had legible handwriting, and even as a child I'd say, 'How do you write like that?' It just wasn't fair. I never finished Year 6, due to breaking my leg at my Holy Communion. I entered my teenage years feeling over-sensitive. I never learned the correct social interaction skills, nor did I feel confident in my ability to write clearly.

The following sentence may seem easy to read. Let's see if you can read it too:

Today is going to be a fabulous day and I feel happy.

Inside my mind it reads and sounds jumbled up and this is what then transpires onto the paper: Today is gon to be a fabulous day and I fel happy. Even when I read through the sentence my eyes become blinded to spelling errors and often I still do not recognise my mistake until someone on Facebook points it out. Being dyslexic is something I just learned to live with and at home I do use a dictaphone and coloured paper is in my printer. The only thing I need to get is rose- or yellow-tinted glasses and I'm all set.

When it came to my learning, I pretty much had to get on with it and left college without any A-levels. That was one of my biggest regrets in life, not finishing my higher education. My dad was the authoritarian type and I always had a shadow of a belief that I was stupid and so I decided to enter the world of work. I went into the customer service industry and was very unhappy because I wasn't living my purpose. I wasn't living my dream. My father was so proud of my sister, who went to college and passed her A-levels with As and Bs. At my default setting, I felt inadequate. Pops (my dad) always ranted on about the importance of education and I would think, well, what university did he go to? All the time he was explaining the importance of a good education and that no one could take it away. To this day, I still feel my dad is deeply disappointed by his children. It pains me thinking about this part of my life because there is so much I would change. However, it did not stop me going on to write 16 books, which led to me developing my own publishing business and to publish the manuscripts of many budding authors.

Being a book publisher by trade means that mistakes in literature really irritate me. It is one of my pet peeves, yet this doesn't make sense because I have dyslexia. The funny thing is, I am actually really good at editing and I am no good with grammar or spelling. I hire freelancers to edit or proofread my authors' books. I have learned to outsource what I cannot do. In business, I have come to understand my weaknesses. However, my dyslexia fuels my creativity, it gets my mind racing at 100mph and I am filled to the brim with creative content and ideas and intellectual property. My strongest skillset is creativity, which translates into many different forms. This is why I have been able to write several books in my lifetime.

I often get frustrated when I don't know how to spell certain words or I cannot sound out words for Google to work out what I am trying to spell. My dyslexia is visual and auditory and I struggle with my handwriting – sometimes even I cannot read the scribble. It is challenging to understand instructions given by those in authority, or by a satnav, or if anyone gives me directions. I always have to plan my route when travelling, otherwise I become anxious. I have to look at the Google map and check the visuals in the area. I can visit a place once I know how to get there by relying on my visual senses, thus I am very good at recognizing landmarks.

To date, I have not let my dyslexia hinder me in business.

What I do not know I learn, or I get someone else to do it.
I think the ability to delegate is a huge plus. I have been
able to write my books because of my gift of writing; that is
what I was given to work with. Do not stop believing in your
talent, dreams, abilities, gifts and always focus on how you
can achieve them. A journey of a thousand miles begins
with one step. My best advice here is to never give up; rest
if you must but do not quit on your journey to your best
self. Being dyslexic is no longer the life sentence it used to
be. Many creative people go on to be very successful, for
example Whoopi Goldberg and Muhammad Ali. There is a
power in being special and different. It means that you are
set apart and you stand out from the crowd, you do not walk
in conformed lines and you can create your own destiny.
So those listening to the sound of my words are encouraged
to keep going, there is so much more for you to explore.
Always look at your cup of life as being half full, and your
job is to make your cup of life overflow, by embracing your
uniqueness before you leave the planet.

––––––

Winsome Duncan, book confidence coach, bestselling author and
publisher.

"Most people don't know what you don't tell them. They can't always pick up on subtle signs. So, I had to go around announcing my problems to every member of staff who would listen in the hope that someone would know how to help me make it through this academic passage. But even after you ask for help, most people don't know how to help.

So, my one tip to my past self would be to learn what I need and instead of asking for vague help, ask for exact solutions. You need coloured paper or tinted overlays? Ask for it. You need questions in advance to give you time to find accessible research? Ask for it. If you need reassurance that you're actually not failing and your writing/comprehension isn't terrible? Ask for it.

It's your time so don't let them waste it looking for solutions that may or may not apply to you.

That's something I wish I'd learned earlier.

I have a feeling some teachers thought I was just being lazy or antisocial, but really it was procrastination due to anxiety of looking like a fool in a room of students who apparently understood everything the first time around. And there is imposter syndrome of being a university student when you still mix up letters and your spelling is atrocious, so you hesitate to take notes unless it's on a phone or computer (ah, but then the people behind me can see my screen and will see how slowly I type or how much I'm struggling... I'll use a voice recorder and take notes later). But later is delayed by two weeks because you have a more pressing assignment due.

Domino effects all around.

Shynell (surname withheld).

Owning Your Dyslexic Superpower

Keisha Adair Swaby

I was born in a little hideaway in St Elizabeth, in sweet, sweet Jamaica but school was a bittersweet experience. We had fun but I had my own secret frustration, questioning myself about so many things. It was hard not understanding so much that seemed simple to others.

I would often wonder why my teacher had to beat me for not knowing or understanding numbers. This particular teacher made my hand sore each morning and I truly believe that my dislike of maths has a lot to do with him and his beatings. I needed to sit by my classmates, who knew what they were doing to try to get the right answers, but that didn't always work. I could copy their work but I couldn't explain how I got the answer. Many times, there was no point copying as I didn't know whether the answer was right and at times they got it wrong and so did I. Then my cover would be blown. The teacher knew I had been copying from the clever one next to me. Some days would be really bad, especially if the usual person that I copied from didn't come to school. Then I would be left in a panic, as that day I would get everything wrong.

While I knew others in my class were also having their own challenges, mine were personal to me because I was the only one who knew what I was going through. These challenges were paving the way for what was to come.

As a little girl, I was a dreamer. Part of my joy was to use my imagination and go to places in my head. I always had big dreams, and when I was growing up in Jamaica I was always excited to escape in my mind to places like Manchester and Brompton in London, where I had family.

All this time, I couldn't have explained to anyone what I was going through. I didn't understand, so how could they? I couldn't pinpoint why I did things the way I did, why I moved slower than everyone else and why I would always drop things and trip over my own feet, or why I couldn't say certain words or even spell them. Spelling is one challenge that I've carried through my whole life. I try, I really do, and a word will look perfect to me but there is always something in the wrong place. It's not right but it looks and sounds right to me!

While I hated maths growing up, I had a love for English, and writing was 'my thing'. I remember writing poems when I was a lot younger and that's something I want to take up again, as I just love using words creatively. I love anything to do with colours and creating things and really enjoyed doing picture mosaics in class.

When I started at my next school, I had the same challenges and they got me into deeper trouble as I became older. I had to sit a test to determine which class I would be placed in. I surprised myself and got a better grade than I expected, securing a place in class 8/2, the second highest. However, my challenges would always pop up and I have so many memories of things that happened that I now know were linked to my dyspraxia. There was the time I dropped the whole bowl of mixture for our food technology class cake – everything went splat on the floor. At that time, I just wanted the ground to swallow me up, seeing all the ingredients all over the floor, after the bowl slipped from my hand, with a loud smash on the white tiles. I felt so ashamed and terrible about it all.

Whatever challenges I faced, I had to overcome them the best way I could, but these challenges were shaping me into the woman I was to become. I retained the hope that everything would become clearer in time. I knew deep inside that I would become all that I wanted to because I was going through the worst to reach the best.

My dream of leaving Jamaica was one I knew would come

true and finally in June 1992, I left for the place I was told had streets paved with gold. I am still searching for those streets today!

England was where I learned to understand why these challenges followed me wherever I went. They were part of me and there was nothing I could have done during my time in Jamaica to learn more and truly understand why I was amazing at doing certain things and not others.

Coming to England was a happy experience. At 14, I travelled on an aeroplane for the first time. Setting foot on the British Airways flight to Gatwick, London, was the true start of the rest of my life. When I checked in and went through to the departure lounge, I was totally confused by all the signs and I didn't have a clue where to go. I had to find a way of making sure I was getting on the right flight, so I looked and observed other passengers that I thought were on the same flight because they were in the same queue as me. At the time, I didn't know what stalking meant but I stalked them all the way to Gatwick where my grandma and my auntie were waiting for me, arms wide open to welcome me to England.

I found everything so different to the beautiful sunshine and food that I was used to but visiting new places was a joy. After the summer holidays, the time came for me to finally start school in the Midlands. It was scary as I knew that the challenges were still there and this school would bring them all out again. It was cold by the time the term started in September. The first day was difficult because, while I could read, everywhere was confusing and I really struggled to remember the names of my classmates. A few days into my new school, I was crying. It was bitterly cold and the children were much more provocative and mean than I was used to. They would get me to repeat things and then laugh at the way I said them. They mocked the hell out of my Jamaican accent and this became their fun at break times (recess). I did all that they asked me to do because I wanted to fit in and not be left lost on my own. I followed a certain group that were part of my class as I knew they were a lot more ahead than me.

School was disappointing in that I left with no GCSEs but I was determined to achieve my English Language GCSE after I left. I moved to Manchester and enrolled myself into Loreto College and went for it. At this time, the challenges were mounting but I was determined and I had an amazing tutor who really helped me. My love for writing got me through and while the challenges were there, I developed my own way of learning and doing things. I knew that I was capable and the belief I had in myself took me a long way.

Starting out in the big wide world of work was hard. My first job came with so many challenges, and every day I made simple mistakes and still didn't understand why. After five years, I was made redundant and had to find another job. Here I still struggled. After leaving to pursue my studies, I found out, after 41 years of challenges, that I had severe dyslexia and dyspraxia.

Everything became clear. I finally knew what was responsible for the difficulties that I faced every day. My life completely changed. My diagnoses fuelled my motivation to make things better for generations to come. I wanted every child going through what I had gone through to receive the support they needed. I wanted every employee struggling and frustrated to have their voice heard, to be in a supportive environment, so they could thrive and be the best they could be. I wanted every student studying, whether at college or university, to be understood and for others around them to know more about their way of doing things and that they might need that extra time in completing assignments and exams. I wanted greater understanding and a lot less shame and embarrassment.

All my achievements – the dreams and goals – none of them have come without their own challenges, but due to my determination, I am on a great journey to help many others, locally and globally, in generations to come. I want others, especially our young people, to see that they too can achieve all their dreams and goals and that their challenges will help them to become equipped with whatever they need to apply to their daily life in order to do this.

As a dyslexic person, I see myself as having many superpowers. I am proud of who I am and how the gift of dyslexia has helped me to be more determined to silence the naysayers.

This quote from Stephanie Fry, Skills Manager for Wales England Care, resonates with me and my journey with dyslexia and dyspraxia and it's one I have to share:

I no longer see dyslexia as a barrier, but as an opportunity to support others in the same way that I was supported to overcome challenges and to achieve my full potential.

I have obtained first class BSc (Hons) in applied sport and exercise science and am currently undertaking a master's in health psychology.

I am on a mission to create more awareness, which is why I founded Empowering Dyslexics, to create more awareness in our black communities and to empower others. I want to use my own lived experience and show what can be achieved, regardless of having dyslexia and being black, because dyslexia is truly a blessing and embracing it is key to navigating the challenges that will come your way.

I am truly grateful to be part of Radio Diamond, which is a great platform to help the mission in reaching people locally and globally.

———

Keisha Adair Swaby, international inspirational speaker, dyslexia speaker, Radio Diamond presenter, Executive Member of Jamaicans Inspired, certified Les Brown Speaker, neurodiversity advocate, named as one of Women Beyond the Box's Top 50 Influential Neurodivergent Women 2022, Founder of Empowering Dyslexics.

EMPLOYED & DISABLED – I CAN'T BREATHE!

Employed & disabled – I can't breathe!

When you deny me access to reasonable adjustment.

When you decide what reasonable adjustment is best for me without consulting me.

When I suddenly find myself in the hot seat of a poor performance procedure and am still denied access to reasonable adjustment.

When you refuse to consider the impact of my disability and the importance of reasonable adjustment.

When you do not understand my disability and refuse to learn about it.

When you use symptoms of my disability to determine or judge I am unfit for the job without referring to reasonable adjustment.

EMPLOYED & DISABLED – I CAN'T BREATHE!

No access to reasonable adjustment – no access to job satisfaction.

Restricting my duties only to my areas of weakness does not bring out the best in me.

When you don't ask how effective the recommended adjustment is but are quick to assess my performance.

When you restrict me to duties that make me look incompetent before my peers all because you delayed my access to reasonable adjustment.

When facts in supervision reports are misinterpreted to make me look incompetent.

When you don't allow a transition period for me to familiarize myself with the provided reasonable adjustment, as recommended, before putting me on a performance plan.

Half access to reasonable adjustment equals no access to reasonable adjustment.

EMPLOYED & DISABLED – I CAN'T BREATHE!

When you judge me blindly for the impact of my disability.

When you put systems in place to deskill me and then blame me for poor performance.

When you are yet to get guidelines from Access to Work on how I can be supported and when the coping strategies I have learnt over the years to support myself are being ignored.

Writing this has been liberating, but please don't condemn me for speaking out.

Some of us feel like we can't breathe because of our invisible disability.

Please help before I stop breathing.

Please help prevent future generations with disability from experiencing the feeling that they can't breathe.

I realize my silence will one day result in indifference for life if I don't speak up.

Please help stop this global pandemic of inequality towards some people with disability.

EMPLOYED & DISABLED – I CAN'T BREATHE!

Uniting as one voice in defence of peace and respect, we can make inclusion a reality, not a statistic.

Thank you for standing up for me – tomorrow might bring another issue, but with zero tolerance to injustice, I believe we can make this world a better place.

Thank you, George Floyd, for inspiring me to speak up.

As your daughter says, 'Daddy changed the world'; your death is indeed making the world a better place.

Rest in peace, brother.

To the hero that recorded the brutality against George Floyd...the world thanks you; as one of the black lives, I thank you.

To me, you are one of the greatest influencers of our time. Thank you!

Eniola Oluwasoromidayo, qualified social worker and poet.

Never Give Up Hope

Dr Tracy Johnson

I worked for years cleaning school buildings for the Philadelphia School District but I knew I had more to offer. I knew I could be more. People around me were focusing on my limitations, not on my potential. I remember one college counselor told me that I should give up but I never  gave up. Even when I was discouraged, I was never defeated, inspired by this quote from Winston Churchill, 'Never, never, never give up.'

I was raised in Philadelphia, Pennsylvania, by a single mother and am the youngest of her three children.

My mother would often say about me that when I was a young girl, 'Tracy taught me how to love and hug.' This shows how my early life was good. It wasn't until the third grade (UK Year 4, aged eight) that my nightmare started, when I began to struggle severely with reading, writing and math. I was pulled out of class and taken to another room to be assessed. I was unaware of what was going on but weeks later when my mother came to the school for a meeting, I discovered my life was about to change forever.

I was placed in special education classes. I was tormented and teased by my former peers every time I went to school. One of my teachers remembers me being terrified as I entered her classroom on the first day. I remained in special education classes throughout elementary school, middle school and high school. The tests they did never identified what type of learning disability I had, they just stated that I was slow in all areas of learning: reading, writing and math. I even struggled in special education classes and was labeled 'slow' by teachers and peers. A high school special education teacher once told my entire class that none of us had the ability for a college education. How dare they dismiss us in that way.

In fact, my dyslexia wasn't diagnosed until I became an adult. Later, I found a tutor to help strengthen my reading and writing skills using the Wilson Reading Program, an intensive and structured multisensory program, which teaches the structure of the English language and how to decode it. This helped me a great deal. Due to my strong faith, mentors, family and friends, I was eventually accepted at

Harcum College where I obtained an associate degree, then a Bachelor of Science from Cabrini College, graduating with high honours.

If I am going to tell you about my dyslexia, I also need to tell you about my biological father.

One life event that had an unforgettable and dramatic effect on me was when I met him for the first time when I was 20. In my neighbourhood, it wasn't uncommon not to have a father around but I still experienced a void and a longing created by his absence.

When I asked about my father the responses were always vague but I never stopped thinking about this mysterious man. In all fairness to my mother, she made a wonderful attempt at being both mother and father to my siblings and me, yet that did little to eliminate the feeling of emptiness that haunted my childhood. I gradually stopped asking my mother questions about him.

Then, when I was older, I saw a television commercial about how to trace long-lost loved ones, and the emotions regarding my father's absence surfaced again. The next day I called the organization but they could not help me because the information at my disposal was rather scant. I was discouraged. A few months passed and I tried to forget about finding my father but it was futile. I was obsessed. I was talking with my godmother on the phone one morning, about my desire to find my father, and she volunteered some information about who he was. 'I'm surprised you didn't know the truth,' she said.

I was shocked at what she had told me about his upbringing and where he lived when he was a teenager. I now knew more. Armed with this knowledge, I decided to become my own private investigator.

I called a few people from my old neighbourhood and met one man who not only knew who my father was but was a close friend of his. In fact, I didn't know it at the time but he had just been talking with my father on the phone. The very next day, I received a phone call from my father. When I heard his voice for the first time, it felt as if my heart dropped into the pit of my stomach, and after talking for a while, we agreed to meet later that day, somewhere in North Philadelphia.

With a feeling of trepidation, I arrived 30 minutes early. Butterflies danced in my stomach. I had an image in my head of what he looked like, that he would have the same eyes and smile as me. I kept checking my watch. Then I saw a very tall African American man walking towards me. He held a long-stemmed rose in his right hand. 'Are you Tracy?' he asked. I replied in the affirmative. He asked to see a picture of my mother. I handed him a picture I had taken of my mother the summer before. His eyes softened. On confirming that I was indeed his daughter, he gave me an enormous hug. In that instant, the void left by the absence of a father disappeared.

Since that meeting, I have gained a whole new family. I have a wonderful stepmother who loves me as she would her own daughter, three stepbrothers and a host of nieces, nephews, aunts, uncles and cousins, all of whom I have become very fond of. We spend holidays together and they support my educational endeavours. My newfound relationship with my father has changed my life significantly because I have discovered the part of myself that was missing and I now feel loved and accepted. My dad and I knew that we could not make up for the lost years, so we resolved to make the best of the years ahead of us.

As it later turned out, my father had not only been missing from my life physically but he was also the 'missing link' as to why I have dyslexia. You see, my father also had dyslexia. All my life growing up, my older sister and brother never struggled with academic challenges like I did. My father told me that he had struggled with reading and spelling in school and how difficult it was for him growing up. After my father and I got to know each other better, he became one of my best friends. I now had someone to talk to about my dyslexia because he was the only one in my family who really understood how I felt.

What I loved most about my dad was his encouragement on those 'dyslexic days' or a day when I simply didn't seem to be able to read or spell anything right, when I was in college. I could always count on my dad to say, 'Baby girl, you can do it,' or, 'I have dyslexia too but that didn't stop me from being a sergeant in the army!' At other times he would say, 'Don't ever let anyone tell you that you can't do anything because you have dyslexia.'

I have taken his advice to my heart. Throughout my life, I have turned my challenges into victories. I overcame poverty despite little support and am now a lecturer and an advocate for people with dyslexia and other learning disabilities. I've been awarded an MA in multicultural education from Eastern University and an Honorary Doctorate of Science in Ministry from the Accredited School of Christian Ministry.

I have founded Vessels of Hope, a mentoring and networking organization for minority people with learning disabilities, and I love inspiring people with dyslexia and their parents and educators and community leaders.

My father has now unfortunately passed away. I deeply miss him for so many things. I miss him most on those really bad 'dyslexic days' when I am struggling – and I have them still – because I could always count on him for encouragement. What made it all so special was that it came from one heart to another!

My father showed me that if he could succeed, I could too – and my message to you, every one of you, is that this is true of all of us.

———

Dr Tracy Johnson, CEO and Founder of Vessels of Hope, President of Harcum College Alumni Association and Minister and Adjunct Professor.

"Always remember that you are unique and you bring value to the world.

Maddie Kamara, retail manager, entrepreneur, podcaster of *Maddie's Chat Show* and *Black Women's Corner*.

10
Be Kind to Yourself

Natasha Gooden

I was around the age of eight years old when I began to notice that I was unable to read and write like the other kids in my class. When we had our spelling test every week, I would get 8/20 correct. From then, I knew something was not right. I never read books at home. In fact, I would pretend  that I had read at home – we used to just tick the books on the list to say I'd read them and hand the list back to the teachers. This helped me avoid doing any reading.

I do remember that when in class, I would try, in my head, to keep up with other children who were reading. I would really want to keep up but I never did. Even now, I am fearful of reading. Due to this fear, I silenced myself and found a way to express myself through dance.

My family heritage is mixed. My Caribbean father, Tony, is black and was born in Jamaica and my mother, Colette, is white and born in the UK.

When I went to high school, I was too ashamed and embarrassed to say anything about my struggles. I did not like my English lessons. I would never volunteer to read out loud in front of the class, as I was fearful of getting words wrong, and I knew I struggled with making sense of the words on the page. I noticed in that moment that I was not able to put the words and grammar together. I was not able to articulate myself very well either.

Fear was so overwhelming and that's when the fear of shame took over – I would notice how the children made fun of people, and I did not want them to make fun of me. That fear is still with me. What masked my dyslexia was my ability to dance and be active.

At the age of 18, I went to Liverpool Community College where I studied dance for two years. This is where I finally asked for help and was tested for dyslexia. The extra help took a huge weight off my shoulders, the weight I had been carrying most of my childhood, and I left college with three distinctions.

The person who made the biggest difference in my life when it came to my dyslexia was Kate Prince, a professional choreographer, writer, director and the founder of ZooNation. In 2011, I was cast in the role as Oprah, the main part for one of her new West End shows called *Some Like It Hip Hop*. This was the moment my life changed for the better.

The show had a narrator telling the story and the rest of the cast expressed themselves through dance, with no words. I found out when having a read-through of the show with every member involved that 'Oprah' had a monologue. You can only imagine how I felt seeing those words on the page. I wanted the ground to open up and swallow me whole. Only that did not happen. I had to read my part out loud in front of everybody. My heart was racing, my palms were sweating. It was a flashback to my high school English classes. The very thing I wanted to avoid came back around to haunt me but this time there was nowhere to hide. So, I took a deep breath and began to read out loud. Once I had finished, a voice in my head said, 'See, that was not so bad,' and I remember being so proud of myself. From that day on, my mental attitude towards myself was so much more positive. I felt motivated. My coping strategy is now self-belief, talking kindly to myself and letting my inner world know it's okay if I get my words muddled up when reading. It's okay if I don't know how to spell a word.

My dyslexic superpower is the word 'believe'. Once I believed I was capable of reading and writing, I began taking action. That day in 2011, reading my part out loud made me take the very action I was too afraid to take when I was younger. I found out that once I had taken that action, I believed in myself and could see so much hope for my future.

My top tips for anyone with dyslexia are to read more and write more. Go back to basics, no matter your age, and start again. If we have dyslexia, we tend to accept the fact that we are unable to read and write at the level we should do, within the expectations of the education system. The point being missed here is we can do it. It's just about self-belief and not being embarrassed about having dyslexia. If I could tell my little eight-year-old self something all those years ago, it would be, 'There is nothing wrong with you. Every child is different and learns at different speeds. You can read and you can write. You just need to work a little harder than the other kids and you will be flying in no time. It's not just about seeing the words on paper; it's about how you feel the words too.'

My biggest tip would be to be kind to yourself and know it's okay to ask for help. Lose the embarrassing and shameful feelings that we allow ourselves to carry and believe to be true. You are amazing and unique to this world and don't let the word 'dyslexia' or any other diagnosis define you as a person. You are here to do great things, and most of all to be YOU!

Now I have an injury, so my physical side is my weakness, but my voice is my strength. I still have the power of my voice.

The most difficult part of having dyslexia is all the negative self-talk that comes with it. I spent my whole childhood thinking I was not good enough and that something was wrong with me. So much self-hate that no one could hear on the outside, just me inside my mind. All this did was to keep me in a shell of darkness that I was too embarrassed and ashamed to tell anyone about. I was too ashamed to admit to myself that I needed help.

I have learned to take away the pressures of English grammar and the use of big words. I have pushed them to one side and instead speak from the heart and find that my words penetrate more. This has led me to be offered the role of narrator in the play *Sylvia and the Suffragettes*. There are 200 pages for me to go through but I believe I can do it.

I was tasked at a recent workshop with writing what dyslexia feels like for me. These are my words:

> Diving deep, into the ocean, behind and within the shell of the physical body, the world that no one can see, the world no one can hear, the world only you can feel.

I used to let what other people said about me affect me. As I have reached an older age, this does not bother me any more.

I now believe it's okay to be different. The colour of your skin is irrelevant, no two vessels are the same. Society makes us feel that we must mimic each other, when it should be empowering difference, not suppressing it.

Society makes you feel that if you cannot keep up with the education system, then you have failed, and this is not right. It is not versatile. There is not only one option. It's not true to say that if you don't conform, you don't fit in, or you are stupid. How dare you say that about me. How dare you say that about anyone.

We need to know our true identity. Stand out and be loud. Dive deep into your own abyss to find out what will help you build your future.

Do not second guess the beauty that is within. We are all incredible human beings. Do not doubt this for a single second. Every moment is precious and not a second should be lost in doubt or fear.

Natasha Gooden, choreographer, dancer, model and actor.

No one told me that dyslexia would impact most, if not all areas of my life. I struggle to read maps and get lost often. I can't think when my mind is overstimulated...and there are times when I cannot find the words to tell you what has caused the overstimulation. I wouldn't change a thing because dyslexia gifted me creativity.

Onyinye Udokporo, CEO and Founder at Enrich Learning, EdTec entrepreneur, educator, public speaker, author, pioneer of social mobility, ranked as one of the Top 150 Future Leaders by Powerful Media in partnership with HSBC and the University of Oxford.

Discovery of My Mind

Antonia Douglas

I was born in the UK to a British-born mother of Jamaican heritage and a Jamaican-born father. I grew up in a single-parent household, when after losing my mother at the age of five, my father became my primary caregiver. He had come to the UK in his late 20s, from

the rural countryside of Jamaica, seeking better employment prospects and life chances.

My first memory of feeling different is when I was reading among my peer group in primary school. In Year 6 (US Grade 5, aged ten), during reading time, in a small subset of the class, we were all given a page to read. I remember hearing others read and hearing myself read. I always stumbled when reading and wondered why I could not read so eloquently as everyone else. I remember when the first Harry Potter book came out, to me it was a huge book. Everyone was reading this book. At that point I thought, well, I don't read books, as I am not like everyone else. I kind of separated myself from others.

Through academia, I became aware of my issues at school. In primary school, I remember scoring really low on my SATs. Through embarrassment, I was reluctant to share my results. I do not even recall telling my dad my scores, as I felt that he may not understand, due to his limited knowledge of the British education system. I do remember that my sister had different support than me from my dad, as she did not have issues with school. I knew my dad was trying his best and did not really understand the education system, so I continued to mask my way through my schooling and just did my best.

I left school with good GCSEs, which granted me entry to my desired college, so no immediate red flags were raised. On reflection, I noticed that one of my friends had a scribe. I thought, 'I want that too.' This is when my friend introduced me to the Learning Centre. Knowing that I needed some support, I took the initiative to seek help.

I did not do well with A-levels (information technology, business and maths). In fact, I failed and I was told that A-levels were not for me and that I should try a different programme. I applied to do a BTEC business course, an alternative programme. Unfortunately, that course was full, so I had to take an IT course, as this was what was available, and I ended up achieving the highest level of distinctions across my year group. The thing is, my dyslexic journey was about me being able to complete things. It was never about how many distinctions I could get.

As I write this, I am starting to see how this was a major achievement for me but at the time I did not see this. In fact, I never really tend to celebrate my achievements, as I tend to concentrate on just 'getting things done'.

At university, after the first semester, I just about obtained a pass mark for most modules. Having gained confidence from school and college to seek help, I was diagnosed with dyslexia in 2012, during my second year of university, following a psychological assessment. I applied for the Disabled Student Allowance (DSA), in which I was able to obtain reasonable adjustments that included laptop and assistive technology. This led to a significant increase in my score. I had a support worker from the first year to graduation and this helped me a great deal. It was my support worker who said to me, 'Getting a 2:2 in your degree is fine. You don't have to be like everyone else.'

I remember changing my university degree three times, before I ended up studying computing and management. I wanted a job in technology and to be equipped with knowledge and skills to enable me to find a job in the 'real world'.

Having dyslexia can be challenging but I was once told that it is not having a disability but rather different abilities. In neurodiverse individuals, uncommon skills do prevail, which for me is my long-term memory. At times, frustratingly, I find it hard to forget difficult life experiences but can also remember cherished memories.

Luckily, the university I attended was very knowledgeable about dyslexia, and about how best to equip students with the right resources, including the support worker and extra time during exams. With these reasonable adjustments, I saw drastic improvements in my performance. Knowing I had dyslexia was a relief but I also knew I had a big challenge ahead.

In my professional life, those around me are not as accepting of the disability. While it took quite some time to be adopted into the world of academia, it was even harder in the traditional corporate world. My belief system always told me that the corporate world would not accept me, so I was afraid to apply for internships and graduate schemes.

If you are currently employed, I would say from my experience that it's important to know what your rights are as an employee with dyslexia and the support that should be made available to you and the importance of highlighting the need for justice. Screening, diagnostic and workplace needs assessments help to secure reasonable adjustments in the workplace. It is also important to understand performance reviews and disciplinary hearings. In one organization, I had to learn very quickly, something no employee should experience with or without a disability. Some disability and equality measures can feel like a tick-box exercise in the workplace.

The workplace has to be the hardest part of my dyslexia journey to date, in the little work experience I've had so far. There have been times when I did not want to go into work, when I felt excluded and as if I did not did belong within the work culture because of my dyslexia. I can feel 'shone upon', as there can be a lack of understanding. Due to my negative work experience, I have sought therapy, which has become an important part of the journey, helping me to find my voice and develop coping strategies in the corporate world. There needs to be a more inclusive way of working to our strengths.

I've had to learn the hard way in challenging my organization and manager who wanted to put me on performance review. This was a very terrifying experience, which can really knock your confidence. All I want to do is come to work and do my job to the best of my abilities, with no judgement, and have the same equal playing field as my colleagues. Talking to family and friends has helped me, especially when I was beginning to experience self-doubt about my abilities and skills.

My professional life with dyslexia needs to come with learner plates, as it can feel so isolating, and a lack of awareness within the corporate sector means that I have been almost frowned upon. I now celebrate the support given at university but, professionally, this is so different, and even with the government scheme Access to Work, as a black woman with a disability there is sometimes no sense of belonging.

I believe that the lack of knowledge of dyslexia in my culture allows for dyslexia to be dismissed and for individuals to be identified as being 'slow'. For this reason, individuals are not equipped with the correct support resources.

Proving to others that dyslexia is a real challenge and improving education around the subject is crucial. Being neurodiverse means that I am different but I am adopted into a community of people who share that same challenge. I do not allow my dyslexia to hold me back from a challenge; I just know I have to work twice as hard to achieve the same goal.

————

Antonia Douglas – Cyber security professional and neurodiversity advocate.

"Regardless of what's going on. Never Give Up. Always speak up and ask questions. If you believe in yourself, you'll make it.

Our family mantra: Manifesting Mark 11:24, Pray, believe, and receive.

Brin and Nial Wilson (USA).

12 Dyslexia and Comedy

Angie Le Mar

I remember from an early age that I could make people laugh.

In the 1970s, there were many power cuts in London and this was a great time for me. This was when all the family would be in one room because we would have to use candles for light. This was my captive audience and it was joke time. I would often pretend to be my mum and my dad.

This was a time you heard laughter and the sound of laughter has helped me throughout my life. Laughter made me feel happy and good about myself. Laughter was like a medicine.

Whenever I was depressed, sad or upset, laughing cancelled this feeling out.

This trasferred to my school life, when laughing got even louder, as I told many jokes. I often joked in class. Everything that happened, I saw a joke in it. Sometimes, I would use jokes to even get out of class, especially when it came to reading, as this was my weakness. I didn't like reading out loud, so in telling jokes, I was told to leave the class. When I was asked to read, I used to think, 'Why did the teachers not ask anyone else to read?' Also, I could not understand how some people could just read. More than that, they could read, look away from the page and return to reading and know where they were. This I felt, was amazing.

Things got bad in school and after being suspended a few times, I was permanently excluded. My girls' school in South London was notorious for having bad students, so when it was known that I got 'kicked out' of this school, I was seen as a bad girl. The thing is, I was 'kicked out' for my behaviour in telling jokes, not for what most people thought – for being in fights. I was accepted into the popular groups but due to my behaviour, I would get suspended again. Drama class became my escape route. Other subjects were, to me, a complete waste of time, subjects like geography and history. 'Well,' I thought, 'why should I care about learning about a map, when I am not going anywhere? Why should I learn about history if this does not relate to me?' I thought that until you (the system) deal with the fact that we were taken for slaves, I am not interested.

Drama became my escape route because I could improvise.
I did not really have to read; it was more about pretending to
be a person. I used to do this as a child and my dolls would be
my audience, so drama was relaxing for me. It felt as if I had
been given a pump that enabled me to breathe. I found the
love for performance.

I remember going for my first audition. I automatically thought
that I was going to 'mess up' the audition because I had to
read, but my 'motto' was, 'you started so you will finish'.
I didn't think the audition went well at all, but I was given
the role because I did not give up. This gave me even more
confidence in myself and was a big lesson for me.

When I was told I was dyslexic, I thought, 'What disease is
this and why did they have to call it something that I could not
read, spell and could only just about say?' I am a left-handed
dyslexic person, which was extremely difficult. Whenever I
tried to read, words seemed to disappear and I realize now
this is why I could not connect with school. In fact, I hated
school.

I began to find out that there were many others who had
dyslexia, even CEOs of large companies had dyslexia, and
I started to understand this and give myself some space.

Having dyslexia did affect me as I did feel as if I was dumb.
I would go to auditions and I wouldn't get the role, so I
stopped going and decided to start writing instead. This was
so surprising because when I wrote scripts and promoted

them to do a show, tickets would always sell out. I found this quite strange as I didn't see myself as a writer. A particularly good friend helped me. I would write and she would type it up for me, as she believed in my work.

This became a massive boost for me. I saw I had a gift. The gift was that I wrote it. The gift was that I appeared in it. The gift was that I learned it and read it.

My great strength came from knowing that Whoopi Goldberg is dyslexic. I thought, 'Well, if Whoopi can do it, I can too.' Meanwhile, I had to turn down roles to host on TV because I realized I would have to read from an autocue and, well, that was just impossible for me. It became noticeably clear that writing and performing was the way forward. Stand-up was the answer and I became the first black stand-up comedian in the UK.

I realized that we cannot all be the same. I do not feel any less than anyone else, just that certain types of work are not for me. On reflection, I was given a hard time at school but I came through it. I had a burning desire from an incredibly young age to make people laugh. I remember going to parties which were called 'Blues', 'back in the day'. In the middle of the party, I would tell jokes and people laughed. For me, laughter showed me, many times, that the hardest moments could become the easiest.

The advice I would give to anyone is, whatever you can keep doing naturally is a gift. The purpose of your gift is to make sure you get it out there and complete it. You will connect with people and no one can tell you that you can't do it. If anyone says you can't come and sit at their table, go and make your own table.

Also, I do not really care what others think of me. Some people think I am too nice or too arrogant. I don't think I am better than anyone. I am happy in my skin. It takes a while, to be happy with yourself. You must tear up all the negative things people told you in the years that have passed, those people that broke your confidence. You need to set yourself to reset and go again. I am 56 years old this year and I am glad God has brought me this far. It takes just one thing to change a situation. I say, whatever you want to happen, get that one thing out of your head. Dictate a different message if you must. Think of something else to become your track record.

Be kind to people. Somewhere, someone is watching and you never know what they are going through. When you love what you do, you will find people who will love it with you. My whole beginning was small and has included some of the best parts of my life. I joined the A list of dyslexic people. Everything comes back around, so stay put, as it comes round like a merry-go-round and you can jump off and use your gift.

I love being a black woman. I understand that the reason I am black is not that I did not get to be white. This was always the plan. I am fabulous. I look at that mirror and say, 'Angie, the award goes to you.' I've always created my own world, a world where I won those awards.

I am in a great space now, confident about my ability and knowing what my limits are. There are some things I am not going to reach. I love reading, I can think, create, and bring my ideas to the stage. I again thank Whoopi Goldberg. A ten-minute interview I was meant to do with her turned into a one-and-a-half-hour masterpiece. I thanked Whoopi and told her, 'When I was young, I saw you. You made me feel that I could do this. As a comedian, I watched you and knew, I want to do that.'

Whoopi looked at me and said, 'Thank you, doll, that means a lot to me.'

I live by the notion 'When you try to hurt me, you are only disappointing yourself.' Always remember your legacy. You are not dumb or stupid, you are gifted. I love people and live by my dad's phrase, 'If I can help somebody while I travel along, then my living won't have been in vain.'

———

Angie Le Mar, British comedian, actor, writer, director, presenter and producer.

"Dyslexia is like a two-sided coin. It has both limitations and strengths. Being dyslexic does not mean you are good-for-nothing. You can be so much more. You have such a beautiful brain to bring much creativity into this world. Look out for the strengths and enhance them. Yes, you can do it!

Rosalin Abigail Kyere-Nartey, dyslexic and Founder of Africa Dyslexia Organization.

The Dyslexic Millionaire

Rod Shields

When I was young, I was called 'slow' and 'thick' and I didn't know I was dyslexic. I wore glasses and my nickname was 'professor' but academically, I was awful. I'd only read about three books. I couldn't memorize things; I remember my parents writing down my times tables and I still couldn't remember them.

I felt I was being stupid. I thought, 'everyone gets it but me'. I dreaded exams but I knew I was very creative.

Fortunately, my uncle was a successful property developer in the US and he employed me to maintain his houses. He was a rich man and influenced me by showing me I could have financial security through property and this was what got me started.

I was also influenced by *The Sunday Times*. I read this even though I was dyslexic, as in it, there were loads of pictures of houses and cars. I discovered that private number plates were valuable. A friend was selling a motorbike with a private number plate, so I bought the number plate for £120 and with the proceeds from selling it on was able to put a 25 per cent deposit down to buy a house. I had wanted to buy a house when I was 16 years old but my family said I couldn't do that. I ended up buying one in London, aged 18 years, for about £100,000 and it's worth about a million pounds now. I enjoy taking an old house and turning it around by renovating it. I enjoy being creative.

Looking back, my entrepreneur mindset started really young. I remember when I was nine years old, I would buy bikes and do them up and sell them to people on my estate. I used to record the music charts and sell the cassettes. I have always been able to make money. The only time I lost money was when I bought new cars.

According to research from the Cass Business School, a high percentage of dyslexic people are entrepreneurs. If I could change anything, I wouldn't. I like my job – being able to buy properties, refurbish them and then sell them, seeing opportunities where others can't by simply walking into a property and seeing things from outside the box.

At school I was good at English literature and my stories were really good. However, then and now I have issues reading numbers. I have to read a number out five or six times before I get it. In the same way, I have to listen to a message five or six times. I have to split it into segments. One long number does not work for me. If someone gives me their sort code, I have to see one number at a time. I can't understand the whole thing. Even if there are three zeros in a row, I have to close one eye and see each zero separately. My times tables skills remain really bad and I have to use calculators at work. I can work out interests and yields because they interest me. I can make good estimations on renovations. I have been doing all of this so long, these skills may not have anything to do with dyslexia.

One of my beliefs in business is that 50 per cent of something is better than 100 per cent of nothing. That's why I go into joint ventures with people. I'm a great believer in collaborating, as I cannot do everything myself. I'm always looking for business partners to do new things with me, even though I have my own structure at work.

Someone once said to me it was interesting to hear my story as their son is dyslexic. My story showed them he can have a normal life and be successful. It is nice for people to know that I can be a role model. You may not be able to do a 9–5 job but you can still achieve. Sometimes, I don't think my dyslexia is really bad, it's something about me that no one can see from the outside but when I mention things and people say, 'Yes, I'm like that as well,' that does make me feel 'normal'.

One of my beliefs is 'You're a long time dead. Live your life. Live for today.' In so many ways, money means nothing, I really do believe that. However, because of things I have done, my son will not have to worry about money. My grandson will not have to worry. I am hoping to leave a legacy for them.

One such legacy is the Black Landlord Group, which I founded to inspire and encourage others. I'm not anti-white but I am pro-black. People have always told me I cannot do things. People say black people cannot do this or do that but I like to support others and prove people wrong. If anyone calls me 'stupid' or 'mad' because of my dyslexia, it does hurt but I'm happy to reply, 'You're the one working 40 hours, I work 12 hours here.'

Rod Shields, business owner, property developer and pre-teen entrepreneur who sold a number plate at 18 years old and bought a three-bed semi to become a landlord. Loves start-ups and thinking outside the box.

" We are judged by a different set of standards.

Being black and dyslexic in predominantly white spaces is a constant source of anxiety, where small mistakes could be misconstrued as signs of unintelligence or worse, reflective of our entire race by those who just don't know any better.

Claud K. Mudimbe, facilitating class action settlement recovery for the Fortune 500 and more in the Argent Settlement Bay Area.

Dyslexia

My Journey So Far

Zoe-Jane Littlewood

I'm a proud dyslexic person on my own journey in life, to spread awareness of dyslexia and to make something more of the dyslexic community. In this chapter, I will share my experience of growing up with dyslexia with a single mother in Birmingham, a UK city full of rich culture and diversity. I will explore the barriers I faced and still face today as a 22-year-old, mixed-race dyslexic person. So, before I can get started with where I am on my journey now, we need to look back at what life was like when I was younger.

As a young person growing up in Birmingham, what I loved

was that there were so many different people. It was very easy to feel that you belonged or were represented. There is a strong feeling you get when you walk around and see people who look like you and may have similar experiences. Birmingham has many rising stars in different sectors of life, from different backgrounds, so it just goes to show we can all do it. However, like most places, Birmingham also has its fair share of crime and underfunding and it's this underfunding which made life difficult, especially in the school sector.

At the beginning of my educational journey, I struggled with reading and writing. I would completely skip sentences while speaking as well as replacing words with completely different ones. Consequently, I couldn't make sense of why I didn't understand certain things in the way that everyone else in my class did. This made me feel left out and, as someone who loves to speak and interact with people, it was really difficult. I couldn't communicate with anyone else in my class because I didn't understand what I was going through. This left me feeling isolated at times, and it was horrible having to keep quiet as no one wanted to talk to me about my feelings.

I struggled with primary school, all the way up to Year 6 (US Grade 5, aged 10–11). My handwriting wasn't great, though I personally never thought it was too bad. However, to my teachers, it wasn't acceptable and I went through most of my primary school using pencils. This left me feeling so left out, as all my friends were using special pens. It was embarrassing. Honestly, all I wanted to do was use a pen to feel like everyone else but it took a long time to get to that point. I also struggled with my times tables and do still to this day. The times tables where you can see a pattern like the 2, 5, 9, 10 and 11 times tables I could do as I work well with patterns. However, I couldn't pick up the other times tables no matter how much I tried.

As my mum knew I was struggling, she would ask for support, yet, due to the school being underfunded, no support was given. My mum just had to watch me struggle and there was nothing she could do about it because despite all her effort, nothing came from it.

Nothing happened until one of my Year 6 teachers spotted that something just wasn't adding up. She could see that I was struggling with reading and writing and that this wasn't matching up with my ability to talk and comprehend. After observing this, she pulled me to the side and started to explain that I could be dyslexic, and that was the first bit of help I received. Sadly, for whatever reason, that particular teacher ended up leaving. However, I'm very grateful that she was the first person to actually listen to me and agree with me that something just wasn't right. This was a big breakthrough for me because someone had finally realized that it wasn't just me being lazy or not trying hard enough. There was actually something that wasn't right.

Now armed with the knowledge that I could potentially be dyslexic, I remember my mum had more talks with people in the school to try to get me assessed and once again she faced the same barrier, that there just wasn't enough funding to get a test. Consequently, I continued the rest of Year 6 knowing I could have dyslexia, but it just wasn't confirmed.

When I went to secondary school, I was lucky that there was a teacher who catered for neurodiverse students, so my mum and I had a meeting with her to discuss everything we knew about me potentially being dyslexic. This truly was the start of my dyslexic journey. The teacher was able to bring someone in to do a screening assessment, which diagnosed me as being dyslexic. I will always be grateful that my dyslexia was spotted at a young age, as I believe this helped me get to where I am now. It did feel as if a weight had been lifted in the sense that there was a reason as to why I was struggling, and for me, I needed this to show others that I was not making it up.

However, I did not know what dyslexia was at the time, which looking back on it, was both a good and bad thing. It was good in a sense that, as I didn't know what it was, I had no preconceived ideas or knowledge of the stigma surrounding dyslexia, therefore I found it easy to just run with the idea of being dyslexic. But it's hard to fully accept something if you know nothing about it, so being told was a bit confusing for me, as teachers had no action plan lined up, nor did they explain to me what dyslexia was. It's hard to be told you have something yet not be given the support needed to work through it. They only focused on the negatives and what I couldn't do, instead of homing in on the positives that come with being dyslexic. One of my most common memories was being told to try harder and to stop daydreaming and, sadly, this is a very common occurrence for dyslexic people and it needs to change.

As I continued through secondary school, I felt alienated because of my dyslexia. I did need the extra time and quiet space given to me during my exams but that then gave me a label. It was a label given to me by my peers, who thought that those who took their exams in a separate room were less smart or, in their words, 'stupid'. This began to promote stigma around my dyslexia. These words were hurtful and the label made it feel as if I was just written off and not worth any trouble. In light of my personality, I was able to brush this off and from the outside, I looked okay, but deep down it did hurt and it wasn't nice.

I would excel in things I had an interest in, for example sport was the one subject where I truly felt I knew what I was doing and that I was on a par with my peers. However, the downside of excelling in one subject and not in others is that teachers naturally assumed I just wasn't trying hard enough in the other subjects. It just goes to show that there was a complete lack of understanding and training around dyslexia.

Towards the end of secondary school, when I received my GCSEs, I was happy as a lot of hard work went into achieving my grades. However, I also felt lucky, as I knew there were many students who I thought were failed by the school and didn't gain the qualifications or skills needed in life. Reflecting on life now, GCSEs and exams generally can set dyslexic people up to fail, as it's all about how well you can remember and retain information. We know that for dyslexic people, this can be a hard task. We need the school system to change and cater to all students, as it is very outdated to place so much emphasis on written exams. The world and technology have improved and are ever-changing, therefore we need our schooling system to follow suit.

When I went to college, I did an extended BTEC diploma in sports and performance. College was a massive improvement for me, as I felt independent and I was able to use my laptop in my lessons, which for a dyslexic person is a big help. I could keep up with the lesson and not worry so much about falling behind, as I was able to type everything up instead of writing everything down. Not only was I able to write my notes on my laptop but I was no longer being assessed on my memory. I had hardly any exams during college, which was a relief. I felt as if everything had changed for the better during college and I had found my voice and confidence in my work, as I was able to take my time with it and use my laptop.

As a dyslexic person, I would definitely say I am creative but more so in sport than arts and crafts. I also believe that because sport was the only lesson where I felt confident, it made me want to follow this path of learning and playing sport. So, during college, I was a part of the netball team, where I was able to flourish and use my creative mind when playing, to gain an advantage. This really gave me confidence and a chance to travel and develop both netball-related skills and skills for everyday life. Just to give one example, I was able to develop my communication skills, as I would always tell the girls on the team what time and where we needed to meet up.

Going to university was a pleasantly unexpected step in my life, as I never expected to achieve this. I didn't believe I was smart enough and thought my dyslexia would make the experience that much harder. I made the decision to go to university pretty late, as I was really happy with my college results and was really passionate about sport and wanted to continue my education on this.

For me personally, university was a great experience and I was able to get the full educational psychologist diagnosis for my dyslexia. This showed I had 7 of the 12 traits, which was pretty interesting. The assessment covered so many bases, such as how many words I wrote and spoke per minute, memory tests, pattern skills and much more. Now that I had this full assessment, I was able to apply for the Disabled Student Allowance (DSA), so I was entitled to a printer and a laptop with different software to help me with my learning.

My main source of support during university was from a tutor I saw every week for two hours. This really helped, as she was able to point out my grammatical errors and help me make sense and get my words on paper for my assignments. My only issue with the university and support was that this tutor had no experience or knowledge of dyslexic people and the way we learn. Therefore, she wasn't able to give me that much support in how I could learn better or what I could do to retain the information I was receiving. However, overall,

I am so thankful for her support throughout my university experience.

Accepting dyslexia can be difficult; it's the first hurdle we dyslexic people come across. Personally, I struggled with this, though thankfully I was diagnosed at an earlier age, so once I accepted it, I was able to grow with my dyslexia to become the person I am today.

I will always advocate for early recognition, as I truly think this is the best way we can help people who are dyslexic. It gives people time to learn what their dyslexia looks like and how it affects them. It gave me time to work out what tips work for me, for example using my green overlay or different speech-to-text apps. These have given me confidence in myself and my ability to write.

However, I will say that accepting your dyslexia is easier said than done. When I was younger, before I accepted my dyslexia, I found it hard because I truly had no idea what it was. It was this unknown thing that for the first part of my life held me back because I knew I couldn't do certain things but no one gave me the tools or ideas to overcome this, so I had to educate myself and overcome this barrier by myself.

Going through what I did growing up, I knew I wanted to make a change but was not exactly sure how to do this. I have always been comfortable talking about my dyslexia but did not know where to take it from there. So, I decided I was going to tell people I was dyslexic and just talk about my experience via social media, as I knew someone would see it and it may help them. This is where my journey started to take off.

I was able to connect with other amazing and successful dyslexic people and we would share our own stories and knowledge with each other. From this, a door opened for me, when I was asked to speak about my dyslexia on other people's platforms, to help spread awareness and target the younger generation. Then from that, more doors are opening and my voice is being heard.

Whenever I appear on different platforms, I'm often asked what my top tips for dyslexia are and I always pretty much give the same response – it's acceptance, education and knowing you're not alone. I honestly feel these three things played a massive role in my life and have made me who I am today. I want to encourage others who may be thinking the same to speak out as you truly never know where you will reach, until you try.

One of my goals, is to showcase that dyslexia does not have to be a hindrance but in fact, a tool, which when used correctly can truly change your life. There has been a stigma about dyslexia for far too long and it's about time we made a change, especially for our younger generation, who are the future. We need to educate them and make them aware that dyslexia is great to have.

In my journey so far, I have met so many amazing dyslexic people and they have helped me to start my journey. I want people to know that there is a space for us dyslexic people out there, we just need to take it with both hands and keep pushing. I truly believe change is coming and that slowly, we are getting somewhere.

I hope reading this chapter has given you some insight into what dyslexia as a young adult looks like and my experiences from then to now. Feel free to follow me on my journey, as I am always looking to grow further and develop with my dyslexia, as well as spread awareness and make a change in how the world perceives dyslexia.

I am already making some big steps in our dyslexic community, so please follow me on my LinkedIn – Zoe-Jane Littlewood and my Instagram – The Dyslexic Movement.

–––––

Zoe-Jane Littlewood, sports therapist, proud dyslexic, BDA Cultural Perspective Committee member.

"There's something so precious about finding people who are 'like-minded', but my goodness, have I had a long and bumpy journey finding the minds like mine! Being an undiagnosed dyslexic when I was younger created in me a profound sense of otherness, which could have been avoided. Being Black in an all-white community, of course, contributed to a level of otherness but the ignorance towards neurodiversity was by far the more damaging to my sense of worth, my own ignorance and the ignorance of those around me, especially when I was a child within an unsuitable education system.

Laura Mohapi, multidisciplinary artist with predominant interest in societal structures and human wellbeing, Founder of Head Of A PinCIC.

15

Life Living

Karinna Brown-Williams

My parents are Windrush arrivals from Jamaica, who came as children with their parents. I am first-generation British. Big family get-togethers, food, music and education were always important.

At school, I always felt I had a bad memory. I couldn't remember my times tables, so I would regularly get told off and be made to stand in the corner, holding one foot and one ear. I think they did this to make me feel as uncomfortable as possible, so that I would get it right next time, which of course didn't work. In addition, reading and spelling some phonic words was hard, particularly those words that children need to know, like 'the', 'were', 'where', 'scissors'. Reading and spelling were okay sometimes. I was better at reading larger words than smaller ones. However, at home if I'd misbehaved, I had to read while one of my parents watched TV and I wasn't allowed to play outside. So, most times, reading felt like a punishment.

I went to school in Germany and Jamaica for a while. I was fluent in reading, writing and speaking both German and English when I was young. The adults around me saw me as quite bright and able. Being able to write, speak, clean, cook, read and always be bettering myself was a standard expectation, regardless of where I lived.

I preferred speaking and spelling to maths. In spite of reading feeling like a punishment earlier on, I used to read as an escape, a way of leaving my reality and entering a different world.

At my UK secondary school, I thought I was stupid, mainly because I took longer to understand things and had a different viewpoint to other people.

Some occasions left a scar on me. One was in English when the teacher announced, 'We are reading sections of the book out loud, taking turns.' I became super-focused, examining every line, side-eyeing those next to me, trying to figure out if they could see my anxiety, the nervous tap of my foot, how I was looking around, checking the paragraphs of the book to calculate somehow when it might be my turn.

Luckily, I wasn't picked to read aloud. I 'accidentally' took the book home, read it, made notes of the difficult words and looked them up in the dictionary. I then started asking the English teacher what book we would be reading next term to get a heads-up and be able to prepare myself for the dreaded reading aloud. Each time I thought of reading aloud, I would become anxious, get a headache, feel sick and sometimes actually be sick. I believe this was the foundation of my self-doubt.

Saturdays were for vacuuming, mopping, stripping beds, washing, going food shopping and homework. Sundays were for helping cook dinner, cooking dessert, more homework and preparing for school the next day. Sometimes I would see my paternal grandmother at the weekend. To me, she was Miss Lou, the Jamaican folklorist, mixed with Nanny of the Maroons, filled with the deep knowledge of Jamaican customs, rhythms, history and stories. She placed value on education and had a deep pride in being Jamaican. If you don't know about Jamaica's education system, times tables are taught from about the age of three or four years old and don't stop at 12 but 20.

Entering my grandmother's house, as soon as you finished saying 'good evening', you would be given a times tables question. The expectation on you to answer correctly was as if this was a million-dollar question. Not answering would result in harsh words, slaps, piercing eye contact and feeling stupid and worthless. I can remember being asked if I was an idiot and being told I must be because of my wrong answers. I remember using my fingers to help me and how anxious I would become. I would regularly leave with my self-confidence completely eviscerated and I started embedding within myself the understanding that I may be an idiot. All this said, I loved my grandmother. She was an amazing woman from the generation where tough love rules. Overall, she taught me toughness, to get up and keep going and not to tolerate foolishness. She planted determination in me and her cuddles were pure love.

I left school with decent grades and then went to college. I always wanted to go to university but thought I wasn't smart enough, so I never made it past researching university courses. I studied management while working in retail, then moved into working in supported housing for vulnerable adults and children. I also worked for the Employment and Asylum Service, until I had my children.

Becoming a parent changed me; I started educating my children early. I became a parent-helper, and the children's teachers were impressed with my three- and four-year-olds, who could read, count, do basic maths and count in twos and threes. My son's Reception (US Preschool, aged 4–5) teacher encouraged, and even pushed, me to do an access to teaching course.

My first attempt at doing the course failed, due to an unsupportive partner. Once my children were in junior school, I attempted it again with more encouragement from the same class teachers, completed the course and was offered places at the three universities I applied to.

When I started university, I was anxious during anything that was presentation-based. Looking back, these were panic attacks. It wasn't until almost the end of my second year that lecturers started telling me they thought I was dyslexic. I had an assessment and was told I had dyslexia, dyspraxia and an IQ of 180. The university gave me assistive technology and nothing else – no explanation of what dyslexia was or what would happen after that.

Even worse, I had nowhere to turn to, to gain clarity in understanding the diagnoses. The lecturers were unhelpful, and the support services told me they had done the assessment so their involvement was complete. Without any support, my mental health, self-confidence and self-worth crumbled. I questioned everything I had ever achieved.

The university advised me to take a year out but, when I wanted to return, I was then told that direct entry was not allowed into the third year. Self-worth in tatters, I left with a lesser degree than I had planned. I felt defeated and like a failure, cast out and branded as not worth keeping, and the feeling of being an idiot returned.

I responded to this by starting to research dyslexia, listing my strengths, and becoming filled with fire and determination that I would go to a different university, gain my degree and work towards my goal of standing up for people with a special need or disability.

My interviewer at the new university asked me to talk about myself and I spoke my truth about dyslexia and dyspraxia. The lecturer encouraged me to do a combined honours degree in early years education with special needs, which gave me a sense of courage, self-worth and understanding. My degree even allowed me to study a module on dyslexia as part of the course. I felt it to be a very negative module, and I found myself challenging the tutor on her beliefs and the negativity being taught.

I did all of this while raising my children single-handedly and ensuring they remained on track educationally. I was also running a childminding business, attending university, planning my weekend so that the children and I did our studies together, doing housework, having family time and keeping up the culture I grew up with, doing things like frying fish and making jerk chicken and curry.

After running my business for five years, I went back into a school setting to work with children in educational environments. I naturally gravitated towards those children with special educational needs and disabilities (SEND) and progressed to working with them in their homes. This was extremely rewarding and the parents were always warm and welcoming to the black woman coming to help them, unlike some of my colleagues. Due to my experiences, I have always wanted to improve things for those with a disability, which includes building on strengths and helping parents to understand their children.

I studied for a master's in special educational needs, to reinforce my SEND knowledge, but at work I experienced bullying, lack of support and discrimination and was denied Access to Work support. This was another place that did not see the value in dyslexic people. First the university, now an employer. I was being bullied, pushed out, micromanaged and my work tampered with, as my Access to Work requirements weren't implemented. My working day was being made unbearable. My health was affected and I was signed off with stress by my GP. The lack of empathy I received for a family emergency finished my remaining amount of patience. I heard a voice in my head say, 'han eeena lion mout tek time tek eeh out cah fi mi workplace cum in lik hell an powda ouse'. This meant that my workplace was endangering my wellbeing, mental health, self-worth, confidence, physical health and that I should get another job and leave.

In my life, my biggest influences have been a mix of positive and negative experiences. These include my different educational experiences, the many things I have learned attending schools abroad, the time spent educating my own children and the encouragement I have received from their teachers. Also, there are the people who discriminate against me while knowing I am more than qualified, able and experienced, and family and friends who have faith in me, push me and encourage me, reminding me of what I have achieved thus far, whenever I have doubts.

Racial biases and being a black dyslexic professional, experiencing discrimination based on my dyslexia – these experiences are not uncommon. It's easy for me to blame myself for some of the things that have happened to me. However, when people who look like you have virtually the same experiences, sometimes down to the comments and events we have jointly experienced in our lives, this shows that the picture is far bigger than any one individual.

Knowing this added fuel to my desire to change the trajectory of the views of SEND, in and outside the black community. I want to be an example of a successful dyslexic professional, to open the community's eyes to dyslexia being a spectrum that has many differences for different people. I want them to know that dyslexia does not limit or prevent success.

I had to take some time to think about my self-worth and wellbeing seriously, and if I was willing to continue in the world of work, experiencing bias, lack of diversity and lack of inclusion of black dyslexic professionals in various organizations. I questioned if I wanted to continue to see children who look like me experience bias in education or if I wanted to make a difference to them. I decided to create Emerald SEND Consultancy, which offers services to families. I also provided training to professionals around SEND. I do contract work across England, working within local authorities.

I would love to say that since I set up my consultancy, I haven't encountered discrimination. I can't. That would be a lie, since the negative views and opinions of dyslexia remain.

Add to this the challenges I face being a black consultant within the special educational needs and disabilities field. Very few of the professionals look like me but nothing deters me and I focus on supporting families of children with SEND in education.

I understand the Caribbean cultural perspective about dyslexia and how to discover your superpowers. I am a professional consultant in SEND and one of my goals is to gain a PhD. I am doing the work I love.

My philosophy in life is that we are all created different, unique and individual. We all have a purpose in life as people with dyslexia. Our foundations are based so much on what we can't do, don't do or don't know. As children, this impacts us across all areas of life, especially our confidence and self-worth, and this moves through to our adulthood. We need to learn about our strengths, go easy on ourselves and take care of our spirit. We need to know that we can achieve whatever we aspire to, if we take small steps and don't just stop, and are adaptable and flexible in reaching our goals. I have come to this understanding because of all my experiences, good and bad, everything I've achieved and lessons learned along the way.

My dyslexic superpower is my ability to see the bigger picture, see what's missing and make the connections required to bring about improvements. I am also a naturally empathic person and I can relate to people's experiences and develop quality, person-centred solutions.

When I feel overwhelmed and stressed and unable to access my thoughts or process them, I don't have one single coping strategy. I step away from what I'm doing and read, listen to music, meditate, watch a movie, or do something relaxing like having a Himalayan salt and magnesium flakes hot bath. Or I just own the mood and say, 'I need to stop, I'm having a dyslexia day; nothing makes sense, this thing is confusing me. I am angry at myself and I need to do something else,' and then I do what my spirit needs.

I've put together a list of top tips to help people with dyslexia:

- Honestly learn about yourself in all aspects: interests, passions, spiritually, desires, superpowers, weaknesses, secret thoughts.
- Embrace everything you learn about yourself – love and accept who you are.
- Know you can achieve your goal, be flexible, adaptable and willing to alter your route.
- Embrace the fact you can and will change, evolve and grow.
- Know in your soul that you can, if you choose to, learn anything.
- Be kind to yourself; planted seeds need time to grow.
- You have superpowers and it is your job to find them, cultivate and use them.
- Do the things you enjoy because that's how you find your purpose.
- Be yourself and enjoy your life.

- Make your own rules and change them if they need to be changed (it is your mind; you are in charge).

Self-doubt can be a continuous personal difficulty that lasts a lifetime. However, you are not simply your childhood experiences, nor your educator's or other people's opinions of you. You are not the eight-year-old who thinks she needs to protect herself all the time. You will grow up to be amazing and successful. Work on yourself. Be comfortable in your skin, in your intelligence, in your beauty because you are important, valuable and special now and in the future. Listen to your soul, spirit and intuition and make them your guiding star.

—

Karinna Brown-Williams, SEND Specialist Director and Consultant at Emerald SEND Consultancy.

"As a black parent navigating the special education process, I noticed the more I accessed *appropriate* dyslexic interventions to remediate my daughter, the less I saw parents and students who looked like me. That was a clear indication of the inequities we experience when advocating for our children.

Winifred A. Winston, advocate, trusted advisor, bestselling author and founder of the *Black and Dyslexic Podcast*.

Going the Extra Mile (Because I Had To)

Stefan Johnson

owing up as a kid, I was diagnosed with having learning delay and speech and language problems from around four years old. This was because I struggled to make full sentences in speech and writing, do basic calculations and I had a slight stammer.

Even though I liked to learn new things, I slowly started to hate school because of being the odd one out, due to my learning difficulties and being a black person. Others were making fun of me for not being able to read a line from a book out loud, or for having a teaching assistant with me for every lesson. I felt like the dumbest person in class and was mocked for having big features and dark skin, especially when it was summertime. That's a lot for a young person to deal with who hasn't even turned ten yet. Right?

At secondary school, even with my shortcomings, I noticed I was still one of the hardest working people in the classroom, just because I was trying to beat or hide my learning difficulties. I did not know I was dyslexic in my early teens. I was trying hard to blend in with society because it was hard enough to deal with what comes with being a black person living in a whitewashed standard, instead of a human standard. Leaving primary school with no SATs and now with no grades higher than C at GCSE really sent me on a low, to the point where I threw my GCSEs results straight in the bin after leaving school to pick them up. I called myself 'The nerd that never got the results' and asked myself, 'How hard do I have to work to achieve anything?'

College is where I started to enjoy learning again and had a sense of value because I could see the possibility of becoming a mechanical engineer in the near future. I loved the learning structure of being independent but also having enough support there if I needed extra time or one-to-one lessons. One of my teaching assistants recommended that I took a dyslexia test because he could see a pattern of what I was finding hard and it turns out I did have dyslexia, which was a relief because I didn't have to think I was just born unintelligent; I just learned and thought differently. I could see that tactile learning and visual learning was definitely something I excelled at, and after four years of studying motor vehicles, I finally felt satisfied with the work that I put in and the results that I received. I even won a Jack Petchey Achievement Award.

Leaving college, I was looking forward to finding an apprenticeship in the industry I had been training for. Unfortunately, that was easier said than done... I joined different agencies and even worked for free for three months (one month at each of three businesses), but I was constantly rejected for being a black dyslexic person and received comments from my employers such as, 'Why can't you read that number plate?' My reply would be, 'Sorry, I'm dyslexic. I tend to struggle with numbers sometimes' and they would say, 'Shut up! Stop lying and just say the plate number!' Or they would say to a customer, 'Oh! Don't worry, my slave can change your brakes for you!' which showed me that quite a lot of employers did not have an understanding of dyslexic people. It also revealed a bigger picture – that I was not seen or treated as a human being in the world where systematic racism and white supremacy are practised openly as well as behind closed doors. This is the system being maintained, even today.

Being a young person, I kept an open mind and thought, 'Well, I always ride and fix my bike, let me try the bike industry.' I managed to get some experience at the bike shop, with a great mentor. He understood the black experience, and showed me how to do new-builds and repairs on bicycles and gave me hands-on experience to the point that I became a bike builder within the shop, instead of just being a sales assistant.

As I wanted to progress with being a bike mechanic, a small independent shop owner gave me an opportunity to become a fully qualified mechanic if I did an apprenticeship for two years with them, so I took that opportunity. The company didn't give me a contract straight away because they said they need to contact a college to do to the application process for the apprenticeship, which was odd. I noticed that the manager of the company used me to serve people of colour specifically. He was presenting an image of diversity which was not true behind the scenes. After all, what's diversity without inclusion? Even though they were teaching me how to do some basic things, I noticed I wasn't officially part of the team and was left out of meetings and not treated as they would treat themselves. Three months later, they decided to let me go due to 'financial difficulties', spending the budget on a new shop. So I was rejected again from the industry – do you see the pattern here?

Even though I moved to another bike shop to earn a living, sometimes I would help friends or friends of friends with their bikes locally. However, it was just a hobby. At that time, I would never have dreamt of owning a business, due to the responsibilities of an entrepreneur and having dyslexia, which don't seem to go hand-in-hand. Even if I could get a business to the point of launching it, I felt that for it to be sustainable and make profit long term, the chances would be less than 10 per cent for me and my capabilities.

Having experienced being treated as subhuman, being overworked in multiple roles, forced to do overtime, I was left with only my tools, business cards and knowledge within me, so I set up SJ Cycles. I had to trust and pray to the Lord that He would guide me to what is right and I put my confidence in Him because I didn't have confidence in myself to be an entrepreneur and make SJ Cycles happen.

Now, here I am! With my own company! From the constant rejection, humiliation and going the extra mile, it has brought me to this point where I have ownership of what I do, so now I can set my own standard for myself and my customers, which was limited in the past. Even as an adult, I am still learning about myself as a dyslexic person and still trying to embrace it but I believe that will soon come, and I'm looking forward to it.

———

Stefan Johnson, business owner and entrepreneur.

"I have suffered or struggled with dyslexia since I was a child. To this day, I struggle with reading long text and processing information from what I've read because of my dyslexia. To combat this, I take supplements which help my dyslexia by improving my cognitive function, making it easier for me to read and carry out tasks. Despite my issues with reading because of my dyslexia, I am a two-times bestselling author. This goes to show that even with dyslexia, you can still excel in your field and become the best!

Makonnen Sankofa, organizer of *The Black Books Webinar*, author and radio presenter.

Healing and Honouring My Way to Dyslexia

Ruth-Ellen Danquah

I believe labels are for jars, not for people; that we should be celebrated for who we are, not just tolerated.

It sounds so simple.

It sounds so easy.

It sounds so basic.

I find that often the simplest, easiest and most basic things aren't always what we experience.

My beliefs about labels stem from what I experienced growing up, and in my chapter I want to talk to you about my heritage, my breakthrough, my assessment, some tips and my current mission.

I am a first-generation, British-born female, with Ghanaian and Nigerian parents, who subsequently created a new culture when they arrived in the UK. They had to create a new life; they did not have a blueprint and had to adapt their values in a new landscape. I was not taught Twee or Ebo; my parents just spoke English. They did not really understand what it was like to live as a black person in the UK. It was almost a culture clash.

Starting from scratch, life was, 'unknown', a new culture related to my parents having to create their own 'world' and navigate a new life. There was no one before them in England to show them the way; they had to build their own networks. Dad was not known in the UK, as he was in Ghana. In Ghana, he had a massive estate and had more status. Here in the UK, it was a 'culture shock', living in a flat, which did not look like the land of Africa.

His father, my grandfather, was Joseph Kwame Kyeretwie Boakye Danquah (1895–1965), a Ghanaian politician, scholar, lawyer and one of the founding fathers of Ghana. He played a significant role in pre- and post-colonial Ghana, which was formerly the Gold Coast and is credited with giving Ghana its name. His mother, my grandmother, Mabel Dove Danquah (1905–1984) was born in the Gold Coast, a journalist, political activist and creative writer and one of the earliest women in

West Africa to work in these fields. She was described by the Ghanaian academic Francis Elsbend Kofigah as 'the trail-blazing feminist'.

Apart from this, which I found on Wikipedia, I know little about my heritage and this knowledge is fragmented, but I do know that my father's lineage were all academics and this made feel that I needed to achieve academically, and his expectations were high.

My parents were divorced when I was young. Watching my mum navigate life as a single mum was challenging because the struggle was real. The default of being in survival mode meant that through the majority of her life, we would experience a burnt-out, emotionally absent parent.

My mum's survival mode resulted in frustration, isolation and trepidation and that was not something I wanted to replicate in my life.

I had to remember I derived from powerful, purposeful pioneers – and that my circumstances may change me but not reduce me.

Writing my own story has set me on a journey to accept, as well as giving me a sense of belonging...

In 2011, a few things happened. I got a triple divorce: a divorce from my husband, a divorce from toxic people and a divorce from shame. It was then that I decided I was going to remove the layers of other people's words that had dulled my life.

They say breakthroughs come in threes, so I took the following actions:

- Enrolled on an accredited training qualification, so I could rebuild my career.
- Joined a public speaking group, so that I could use self-expression to provide exceptional ways to influence others.
- Strengthened my spiritual practice, so I could do much-needed shadow work, to get in touch with deeper sides of myself.

It was messy and liberating and took courage to continue what I started, especially as every step I took was scarier than the last.

I have never liked the word 'diagnosis'; it always sounds so final. While doing my teaching qualification, I discovered that the college was offering assessments for dyslexia. As you read this, especially if you identify as dyslexic, you will know that self-discovery is the beginning of the journey. I was diagnosed in my thirties and it wasn't the best experience, to say the least. I recall being cooped up in a dingy room, with extremely uncomfortable seats. I told myself that I should never ever be arrested because I imagined this was just as intense as an interrogation gets. I had the feeling that I had to become the 'strong black woman' in the moment, due to the level of disregard for my feelings. The story of my white counterparts' assessments years later was far removed from mine. It made me wonder whether this is how the black experience of dyslexia differs.

I was asked questions about my childhood that seemed so irrelevant. I only recall 10 per cent of my childhood experience, which wasn't a good one; my upbringing was traumatic. I couldn't tie my shoelaces until I was ten, I didn't have good bladder control and I literally had only a couple of friends. I remember hearing my sister telling her friends that I was not normal. I always wondered why it was incredibly challenging to make friends.

I wanted to connect with others but it was inexplicably hard. It's almost as if you want to speak but your mouth has been stapled together. I was highly sensitive. Decades later, I was to find out that this was a combination of dyspraxia and dyslexia traits. These learning needs were not accepted in the culture I grew up in; I was punished for exhibiting these traits and I vividly remember the red shoe my mum used to beat me with.

Knowing what I know now and with the insight I now have about dyslexia and dyspraxia, I may have managed to convince my parents that I wasn't making excuses. But to this day, my dad thinks that fish oil will cure my son's autism.

I was called names and made fun of. I learned to defend

myself, thanks to my mum's interesting disciplinary tactics.
I felt as if I didn't belong anywhere and maybe I could have
been okay with that, accepted it more, instead of having
feelings of unacceptance. My parents took a step back and
were uninvolved in my education journey. It was almost as if
they gave up on me. I spent countless years crying because I
couldn't figure out maths. However, with the help of my sister,
who was a couple of years older, I passed my exams and
enrolled at a college where I studied hard. My self-esteem
finally improved at the age of 34 years.

While one might expect that the biggest challenge is the
diagnosis, I found the lack of support from people who were
supposed to have my back more challenging. Over the years,
I have channelled my negative experiences into working hard
and learned lessons along the way. The challenges I faced
drove my determination to excel in what I am good at. I went
on to found the peer-to-peer network Dyslexic Success and
qualified as a PTLLS ('Preparing to Teach' in the Lifelong
Learning Sector) educator.

As I grew up not knowing I was neurodivergent, I developed
coping strategies which meant I had to learn ways to figure
problems out; there was no getting around them.

I looked at the world as if everything had a solution. It's how
I built resilience, and the situation with my diagnosis was no
different.

I saw an opportunity to help others, so I started a network for dyslexic and neurodivergent people and deep-dived into the world of intersectional neurodiversity. The network I created had psychologists, entrepreneurs and academics delivering their insights and 'selling' from the stage. The value here was in learning not only from one's own mistakes but from other people's too.

I am a trainer, delivering workshops within the neurodiverse space. I became a Neuro-Linguistic Programming (NLP) master practitioner, a certified life coach and a Crystal Reiki Master. I have coached leaders within companies such as Rio Tinto, an Anglo-Australian multinational and the world's second-largest metals and mining corporation.

I have worked in sales for over 20 years, during which time I managed to accumulate over £120 million in new business. I am a believer that within the dyslexia community, we can empower each other by sharing our skills and talents. I also believe that once we accept and embrace who we are, we can tap into our superpowers and celebrate our talents and successes. My message to fellow dyslexic people is that once you set your mind on something, go for it. Don't let dyslexia own you, own your dyslexia. It is important to honour who we are as we will meet many people who have intersectional challenges too, with similar but unique experiences. Ultimately, the diagnosis rarely means anything; we know ourselves more than any test.

For me, my dyslexic superpower is probably mixed with my dyspraxic superpower and that is being able to pick up concepts really quickly. I have learned to regulate my emotions by cultivating practices to strengthen my faith, using meditation, mindfulness, implementing cognitive behaviour therapy strategies, spending time reflecting, and utilizing technology.

___

Ruth-Ellen Danquah, neurodiversity consultant.

" Gaining an understanding of my dyslexia allowed me to improve my artistic practice with simple things like more audio books that are 400-page novels.

Roger Robinson, TS Eliot Ondaatje Prize-Winning Poet, Fellow of the Royal Society of Literature, alumnus of The Complete Works, collaborator on The Rest Residency, and musician.

Beyond Obstacles

Grace Macarthy

My family heritage is Black Sierra Leonean with some white French-Swiss ancestry on my maternal side. That's where 'deloes' comes from, originally spelt, 'de Löes'.

Academic expectations from parents from Sierra Leone are incredibly high and their willingness to recognize but also accept special educational needs (SEN) can be limited, if not non-existent. Black African parents are also very competitive within the community and there is a massive and irrational stigma around SEN. Often, underachievement is put down to laziness or poor effort or being due to poor parental guidance. So poor academic results are blamed on both parental influence and the child's engagement in education.

My mother suspected in primary school that I was struggling and flagged this up numerous times with the school but it was overlooked throughout my primary and secondary education, resulting in very poor GCSE grades with the exception of a grade C in childcare – my true calling. This underachievement made me feel inadequate and embarrassed. It did not teach me resilience but rather to keep quiet and be passive, as a way to avoid exposing myself to others.

Fortunately, my learning difficulties were picked up in college and it was here, aged 17 years old, that I was assessed and dyslexia diagnosed. At last there was a reason for my academic problems and I wasn't stupid. However, a lot of damage to my self-esteem had been done at this stage and I was significantly behind my peers.

I went on to work in retail, which was okay, and then I had my first child. Once she started nursery, my passion to work with children was reignited and I got a job as a nursery assistant, where I worked for a year. Then after speaking with my sister, who is my biggest cheerleader and inspiration and believes in me more than I do myself, I enrolled on an Access to Further Education (FE) course so that I could go on to study midwifery in higher education. I completed my FE course and secured a place at City University. My first year was tough but I passed it; however, in my second year, I met another hurdle. Rather than take the additional support given to SEN students, I decided to go it alone. Sadly, I failed the same assignment twice and lost my position on the course. My appeal was unsuccessful too. This does bring me some sadness and disappointment in myself.

I later went on to have more children and work as a teaching assistant with SEN pupils, which is rewarding but not as much as I know midwifery would have been.

My dyslexic superpower relates to my meticulous organizational skills. I organize things weeks in advance, considering how plans could work out in different ways, so that I'm prepared for any changes that can occur when I'm going shopping, taking the children on holiday, going for a job interview, going somewhere I've never been before, completing a form or doing anything else. I also have my eldest daughter spellcheck much of my written work.

Despite the messages that came from my childhood when I struggled with school life, I would now tell my younger self that I am special, intelligent and capable. I would ignore the limiting career advice I received from my teachers and take any additional help that was offered, rather than trying to do things unsupported, especially during my further and higher education journeys.

The most difficult part of my journey has been doubting my ability to read and write, as this caused me immense anxiety and, as a result, I shied away from meeting people, for fear of appearing stupid. It kept my career goals minimal and ill-navigated because I lacked any confidence or self-belief to truly pursue my dreams. Completing applications or conveying my ideas or work in written form is still a challenge for me. As a child, I felt as though I was living in my sister's shadow, constantly comparing myself with her academic application and achievement. I wish I hadn't done that. We all have our own strengths.

As a mother, I make sure I'm able to support my children with their schoolwork. Sometimes I worry that my children have dyslexia. This worry is irrational but it's still a deep concern for me, as I don't want them to experience what I did and still do. It's a constant battle for me.

———

Grace Macarthy, proud homemaker and mum.

"Dyslexia has always been the whisper behind closed doors. The secret you dared to share. It has now become the thunderous pulse of society. So, whether you are a parent, educator or self-advocate, you will find that your voice that was once hushed has become a roaring call to action. Every classroom, technology company, healthcare facility and government sector requires your narrative. Be deliberate as you share your dyslexia story.

Jeannette Roberes, MEd, Chief Academic Officer Bearly Articulating, speech therapy and dyslexia advocate.

18

My Gift to Dyslexia

Dr Leonie Campbell

I am a black British Caribbean female, born in the city of London and I've worked in the field of psychology for the last 17 years.

Having gained experience in psychology and understanding social constructivism, I believe that in order to support clients and problem-solve, it is imperative to understand their perspective. As such, in terms of dyslexic employees in the workplace, although there are phenomena that employees face due to working in the UK, individuals will experience encounters at work that will be personal to them.

I went to what I would consider to be a very good primary school, which allowed me to do amazing things – performing arts and acting, playing to my creative side. Additionally, I was also excelling academically and was encouraged this way. I think that having such a positive start, where I was surrounded by practitioners who could identify what people were good at, regardless of whether their talent was mainstream or not, really helped me to be more confident but also meant that it did not seem to matter whether I or my peers at this age were neurodiverse or had any difficulties. The school played to our strengths and ensured that these were capitalized on. Over the years, I have grown to appreciate this, as through work and education, I have always felt confident to try my best. I learned from a very early age how to articulate myself to the world. If we don't get to play to our strengths, we can struggle and not have our time to shine.

When I was at university, I always knew that I worked hard and understood information differently from my peers, so I went to explore having a diagnostic assessment, where my dyslexia was confirmed. I spoke to my mum, I think I was in my late twenties, early thirties, and when I told her, she did not comment. Mum told me from the start that she did not accept that I'm dyslexic; she knows I'm quite bright and I've always been at the top of my class, so it was difficult for her to accept that I could have any form of learning difficulty because she did not consider me a poor performer or to be struggling in any way.

I think this has been one of the biggest challenges of being dyslexic, not having a story to tell, that I was struggling in school or through education, like many would expect.

I have realized that because my dyslexia is hidden, when I unveil it, people still find it hard that I am showing it and may want to talk about it. Dyslexia has given me a strength of character that is really necessary at times. There have also been instances when I asked for assistance, not because of my dyslexia but because I needed some guidance, and it was maybe portrayed as being linked to my dyslexia, when this was not the case. I find this difficult because people may choose to work with me because they feel they won't need to support me.

However, over the years, I have come to realize that people need to accept my strengths and development opportunities like everyone else's, because nobody is perfect. For these reasons and many others, I've realized that being neurodiverse gives me compassion for myself and empathy with others. I really have understood the importance of being kind to myself.

Through running my own private practice for many years, I've learned that I have to recognize my strengths and opportunities, which usually means having hard discussions about what I cannot do and what I need others to do to support me. I will write a discussion down or write a diary entry, making it clear what needs to be done because without support, I won't remember when appointments are, or when certain things need to be done. Therefore, helping others understand what is important to me, what my needs are and how we can meet in the middle is what helps me.

Being the guru of myself and being able to tell people what I want from them and what I can deliver, rather than focusing on what they are not doing, works best for me. This can be difficult, but I make it positive by thinking of how we can work better together. The minute I have this type of self-talk, the negative sort of outlook where I think I'm not good enough begins to disappear. This is a work in progress, but we have to start somewhere. I have learned to not hide, not to pretend that things are always easy.

Dr Leonie Campbell, occupational and counselling psychologist.

" I believe that as a group of people we can and should say that we have safely arrived at a place where we can take a positive stand in the comfort and knowledge that *we are indeed capable people, very capable people* and remember that it is just our brains that *work or think differently, that's all! And then go on to remember that that's no bad thing!*

Dee Davis, TEFL, Cert FE, Dip Career Coaching, BA.

Lost,
Now Found

Alex Onalaja Jr

I was misunderstood in school and seen as a student who wouldn't amount to much in life. The lack of awareness of dyslexia, at my time of schooling in Nigeria, was one reason. My culture didn't believe such a condition existed; they just believed you must study and work twice or three times as hard to catch up, or to be better than your peers.

I rebelled against the academic system for as long as I can remember because I just didn't fit in. I continued to attend simply because my parents were adamant about completing school to at least degree level, but I grew up feeling like I had been put in a locked box, locked in another box, then wrapped with a ribbon labelled 'lazy and incompetent'.

When I came to England, I was sure this would change, as I believed there was a better schooling system, but to my surprise, the condition wasn't identified until I went to university. I was diagnosed very late, during my last year at university. I finally knew why I had been struggling to complete simple tasks that others could do in minutes. In short, going to university saved my life because I was settling for less up until that moment.

As I grew older and became more aware of my condition and its strengths, I began to appreciate it. It became clear to me that I was gifted in a way that meant I could see the world differently and as a result, I could bring change to the world. My dyslexia superpower is that I can see the successful outcome of most things and my duty is to guide others through my vision to it.

My late grandad had this good old saying, 'If you are a turtle and your competition is rabbits, while they are snoring zzz, start running.' These simple words and his unconditional belief in me, even when I couldn't see past my undiagnosed weakness, gave me strength to pursue my wildest dreams.

I have four coping strategies now:

1. I don't bother myself with people's judgement or perception of me. Why? One of the most common

mental challenges for people with this condition is stress and anxiety from the frustration of not being able to communicate or express their thoughts or emotions.

2. I trained my brain muscles to work hard, not to the extent of sleep deprivation but by managing my most valuable asset wisely: my time. I have learned that dyslexia can present a mental challenge of trying to 'be more', so this is crucial.

3. I made writing and reading a hobby. As much as I dislike reading and writing, I have learned to drive myself to do it daily, as a therapy to master how to express my thoughts. It has helped me become an author and writer for a few global business publications and personal development magazines and sites. One of my books – *Lost, Now Found: The Secret to Unlocking Your Hidden Potential in 30 Days* – inspired the title of this chapter. The book is a personal development guide tailored to help people find their calling in life.

4. Lastly, I surround myself with people who possess incredible skills in areas I recognize as weaknesses, and I learn from them. This includes my partner, mentor, coach, friends and colleagues.

People who have dyslexia are great at problem-solving and focusing on the larger picture – no wonder they make prominent business leaders. A study of self-made millionaires in the UK, commissioned for the BBC television series *Mind of a Millionaire*, found that 40 per cent were dyslexic.

The integrity of our efforts should not be limited to our neurodiversity; it is who we are.

——

Alex Onalaja Jr, featured on Forbes, named in the top 50 inspiring, prominent and influential Black voices in UK Black Tech by Tech Nation, entrepreneur, author, speaker, mentor, Black dyslexic, contributor at Global Business Playbook.

"Dyslexia in the streets

I am black and unseen, my cry for help is ignored by teachers.

I know there is something not quite right, my parents are confused, and punish me, like the teachers in school. They believe them, even though I ask for help.

My frustration runs deep, and my anger grows louder, as I witness the unconscious bias within the education system.

Is it my colour? Or could it be I am stupid? My thoughts and feelings merge into a ball that leaves me confused.

I run into those that are like me and we play cops and robbers in the streets. This is my life, my dreams and aspirations of an education are now beneath me, I am now finally seen by others like me... The streets are my education.

Gary Baron, MA in Child, Adolescent and Family Psychotherapy, PG Diploma in Psychosynthesis Counselling, Advanced Emotional Freedom Practitioner, NLP Diploma, Reiki Master, Diploma in Sandplay Studies, AAMET Registration, MBACP, UKCP Accredited Register.

The Only Way is Up, From Ds to Dyslexia

Lucita ComWillis-Paul

I first discovered I was dyslexic when I went to college. Due to my low GCSE grades, I was told that I could only do a foundation course in leisure and tourism. I'd set my sights on doing an intermediate course and felt disappointed. I knew I'd find the foundation course too easy. I could do better than that. However, I knew my grades were concerning and I was subsequently referred to the learning support department for a functional skills maths and

Photographer: Anna – *HEARDinLONDON* https://www.heardinlondon. com. Photo Journalist & Street Photographer. Photo shoots for self-esteem, body positivity photography, Transition photography.

English assessment, to identify any educational needs that I might have.

I recall asking the woman who assigned the course, what was the best grade anyone could achieve on the course. She said that it was a distinction and I responded that I would get a distinction and when I did, I would come and show her. I wanted to prove to her that I could do better than this foundation course.

Initially, college was not how I hoped it would be, but it turned out to be the best educational experience I've had to date.

The skills test I was asked to complete by the learning support department showed great disparity and indicated that I was most likely dyslexic, although the test was not conclusive. I was sent for a formal diagnosis test and the report came back that I was what was then called a 'high-functioning' dyslexic. This was a eureka lightbulb moment for me. After years of struggle, self-doubt and emotional trauma, I finally had answers for what I'd been experiencing. There had been this huge obstacle all this time and now I know what it was. It had a name.

I felt that I'd now been given a lifeline and I was in a place that had the resources to help me navigate this situation and show how I could work with it. In that moment, I can say that I was truly happy. A few weeks later, I felt sad because, in my eyes, I had been failed by so many teachers in the past and failed by the system too. I was upset about all the time I'd lost. Although after this, to be honest, I was a happier, more empowered young woman for knowing that I had dyslexia.

My personal development continued. The college I attended in North London was forward thinking with its dyslexic support, even though at this time my spelling ability meant that spellcheck couldn't recognize most of the words I typed. The college had an IT suite with computers that had talk-to-text technology, scanners for books, access to recorders for note-taking, and staff who supported students who accessed the room. The college also provided one-to-one sessions, to teach me learning strategies.

I was excited. It was wonderful to have tools, tech and people to support me at this time. I dedicated myself to my studies and I passed that foundation course with a distinction, just as I said I would. I spent a further three years at college and passed the intermediate with a merit. I completed the travel and tourism course, to the highest level. It was a proud moment for me. The affirming moment of college was the final class project, which was a group activity. We decided to put on a conference and the class had to nominate a project leader and they chose me. It was a good feeling and a sign of the distance that I had travelled with dyslexia.

My first experience of coping with dyslexia in a challenging environment took place in my first job in a fast-food restaurant in Camden Town. I had good spoken English, so I was asked to work on the tills. The manager who hired me saw potential in me and I began working part time, as it was a summer job. I was there for three years.

The problem was that my mathematical skills were not very good and I relied on the till to do the mathematical calculations for me. I would input how much money I was given and the till would let me know how much change to give a customer, as I didn't really know.

At times, this created situations at work that were uncomfortable, for example a customer might purchase food that came to £5.15 but present me with ten pounds. If I used the till, it would say what the correct change would be, but if the customer then gave me the odd 15p when they were paying, I would not be able to process this mentally and it led to me giving back too much or too little change. My till would be up by too much or down by too much. The manager who employed me had left and I had a new manager and, at one point, I was going to be investigated because they felt that I was stealing from the till. It was so unfair.

Many years later, I heard about a case with a dyslexic person who was having issues with money-handling at a well-known coffee shop. Thankfully, they won the case that was brought against them. I was so happy to hear that because that was the situation I had been in and I didn't know how to tell them, as I was scared to discuss my dyslexia, not recognizing at the time that there was a connection.

Thankfully, my uncle's wife saved me from being sacked

when she gave me the opportunity to fill a short-term post. She needed a project worker for 12 weeks at the charity Women Mean Business, based in East London.

I was given an outline of what she needed. I went to meetings to promote our projects, I wrote reports, sent emails and made calls. I had the opportunity to be creative, designing posters and flyers. I was also able to utilize the skills I'd gained at college. I had to learn how to use an A–Z map, as there was travelling around London and these were the days before smartphones. I found this challenging, so would call ahead to ask for directions and, most importantly, I'd get visual landmarks, like knowing there was a post office or postbox on the corner. I found it extremely hard to follow directions such as 'Walk down to the end and take the first left, then the second right', as I struggled to process this information. I was learning more about my dyslexia all the time.

The wonderful thing about this role was that I was alone in the office, which meant I was able to create my own environment. I would play my music and I could talk out loud to help me think. It was this role that led me to youth and community work. After I had completed my three months there, I went back to my old youth club and asked the manager, Cheri Class, if I could work for her. She gave me the opportunity to work on a voluntary basis and this experience encouraged me to go on to study at university.

Going to university was a bold move. No one in my family had been to university. My mum was supportive but my dad was fearful for me. I knew that I could do it if I applied for Disabled Student Allowance (DSA) to obtain dyslexia support. The support in terms of the equipment was good but one-to-one was not so good. I set myself a goal of doing the best that I could and I went all out, using skills and strategies I had already learned from before. I had colour overlays and I read on the bus, as I had long journeys every day. I found I needed dialogue and to discuss what I had read with someone else, so that I could understand what I was learning, so my friend helped me with the content, although she was not knowledgeable about my subject. By sharing with her, I was able to make sense of what I had learned and enhance my own learning. This was another strategy I had learned to help me tackle my dyslexia.

The degree took me three years to complete and it was not easy. In order to complete my dissertation, I did have to pay for help. Ultimately, I achieved what I had set out to do and completed the course, gaining a 2:1. This was a proud moment for me.

Achieving this helped me become stronger as a person. It showed me that dyslexia is a barrier but it can be overcome with hard work, the right support and tenacity.

While I was at university, I had a part-time youth work role with a local authority. When I graduated, the local authority was going through some significant changes in how it delivered youth work. They trained me in those new techniques. I was actively encouraged to apply for a full-time role and they gave it to me. At that time, applying for jobs was pretty straightforward, whereby you completed an application, made a skills statement once you were shortlisted, and had a face-to-face interview in front of a panel, for which you may have been asked to prepare a presentation. I think this type of interview process is fair and requires everyone to do a bit of everything that would be part of the role they were going for, with no test, and I was able to compete in this setting with little need for reasonable adjustments.

So, at 25 years old, I became a senior youth worker. This placed me in a supervisory role, leading a small team of part-time youth workers. I had to ensure that all paperwork was completed to my employer's standard, such as risk assessments, quarterly projections, weekly session plans, registration and evaluation of young people. This role was a big 'step up' for me. While I was happy to have gained such a role, fresh out of university, the size of the task ahead of me was intimidating. The team I was leading had a mixed age range from 26 to 50 years and there were high expectations.

I now knew what I needed to help me carry out my role to the best of my abilities. I applied for Access to Work support and I was awarded talk-to-text tech equipment and a recorder for note-taking. These tools did help but in this new role, I found it hard to manage my time. I took the leader role very seriously but I didn't quite have the skills to motivate and encourage staff to do the tasks they needed to do and found myself in situations where I was doing most of the work for my team behind the scenes, as well as supporting staff from different teams.

I had very little support from my manager during this time, I was doing extra hours over the weekends, I was stressed and this led to disorganization. Having structure and order was a key part of my coping strategies and after a year of working like this I started to become burnt out, yet I stayed for another two years before taking voluntary redundancy.

I took six months off work to recover.

Then, through an agency I gained what was meant to be a short-term role in a large further education college. There was no formal interview process, just a face-to-face meeting with the manager, where I was able to sell myself and my skills and was given the role as an agency staff member to cover someone's maternity leave for a few weeks. The role, as face-to-face youth worker, was to support students to remove barriers to education and ensure they adhered to the student code of conduct. At first, I was just covering and didn't do much paperwork. I was then asked to cover the whole maternity leave and I jumped at the opportunity.

When I took on the role formally, the paperwork and the demands of the job increased. I had to work harder, including at weekends. I put in time when no one else was looking and again experienced burnout. I knew what I needed to help me, but was unsure of who to speak to about my dyslexia. I didn't want to appear dishonest about not disclosing my dyslexia sooner and I didn't want to show that I was struggling to cope but here I was in need of another lifebelt, as I was starting to drown.

At the college, there was a team that dealt with young people who had learning difficulties and they encouraged me to speak up and get the support that I needed. I informed my manager of my difficulties and talked about the technology that I needed to help me to do my job at the same pace as everybody else within my team. I explained that I needed my own computer, as we were sharing them in our team and we had a significant amount of paperwork. Due to my lack of speed, I was slowing the process down and these issues had started to affect the team and were causing friction.

My manager got me a Read & Write Gold portable on a USB stick, without applying for Access to Work. While this was a helpful tool, I needed more. I made a formal application to Access to Work and 12 weeks later I was awarded *Dragon Naturally Speaking* software and some training in using it, work/time management strategies, coloured overlays and a stenographer. This transformed my ability to do my role and stopped me from suffering continuous burnout.

Through this experience, I realized I would have to consistently speak up for myself as a dyslexic person. It wasn't worth me hiding it because it meant I had to work twice as hard as everybody else and that would most likely lead me to burnout or worse. I was dyslexic, now and always.

I have the right here in the UK in every setting I'm in to ask for what I need to succeed.

I continued in this role for another five years. Other people that joined our faculty team expressed to me that they were dyslexic and were coming under harsh criticism for making mistakes. I informed them of the law and what they needed to do in order to secure help and support.

This is when, as an adult in the workplace, I started to become an empowered dyslexic person.

Looking back, I think Access to Work is really good but the process is long and as the equipment is awarded to the organization, when an individual leaves they must leave the resources behind. The system of support for dyslexia and other neural diversities needs to be updated for the new way of working and individuals should be able to take the resources they have been awarded with them, from job to job or role to role, without needing to do the whole process every time. This would give power to the individuals and allow them to be flexible in the work environment, which is so very key in the world we live in.

I believe that growing up in the mid-80s and 90s meant that as a young black female, I wasn't necessarily seen as someone who could have had a learning disability and this is why it wasn't picked up until much later. Within my community, I have experienced both understanding and a lack of understanding. Thankfully, my family accepted the fact that I was diagnosed with dyslexia and greeted it with as much joy as I did, as it provided a solution to the problems that I was having. From other sections of my community, I've been told that I just need to read more and that stating that I'm dyslexic doesn't help me to progress.

I'm glad that we are now living in a time where more people from my community are beginning to accept that we do have different types of neurodiversity and that there's no shame in this. With knowledge, understanding and support, people can succeed.

––––

Lucita ComWillis-Paul, qualified youth and community worker and educator.

"Over the last ten years of teaching students with dyslexia and other language-based learning differences, I learned very quickly that these students believed they weren't smart mostly because of environmental circumstances and lack of knowledge about what supports and accommodations were needed. Once these students were taught in a direct, explicit and multisensory way, they were able to unlock their true potential. A whole world of confidence and excitement opened up and they began to realize just how intelligent, capable and hardworking they truly were, but just needed the right approach to get there.

Dr Lauren McClenney-Rosenstein, Founder of Think Dyslexia, Orton-Gillingham specialist A/AOGPE.

Resilience!

Alice Aggrey-Orleans

When I was four years old, I moved to Ghana from the UK, where I was born. In the 70s, no one in Ghana had heard of dyslexia and school there was tough.

I struggled with maths, reading and writing. I was called 'thick, slow and stupid' and grew up believing I was all of those things. I believed what I was told by teachers and family members. Growing up there, it was like they had pity for me. The message I was receiving was, 'This child is not bright, so what do we do with her?'

Every day, I had maths and a teacher would come in and we had to recite times tables. I could not do this. I would stand up and just move my lips, to pretend and blend in. The teacher would 'sus' (catch) me out and I would get caned with a ruler every day, with the side of the ruler. The teacher would hit the tips of my fingers. I cried, but I got used to it. When I went to maths I would take my hand out ready for the cane. I knew it was on its way.

French was difficult too. The teacher would take a pen and pinch the inside of my arm and rub it. It was so painful. I hated school. The word that sums it up for me is 'traumatic'. I remember wishing I were like my siblings. I just thought they were brighter than me and that I was not going to amount to anything.

Then I came back to the UK at 12 years old and went to secondary school, a high school in north-west London.

As I was 12 years old, I missed the first year. The year head sent me straight to the second year (US Grade 7). Everyone had already made friends so this was not a good experience. I was bullied by the black school kids for being African. They told me to 'Go back to Africa' and called me 'booboo'. I believed I was thick as that is what I was told. I couldn't even tell the time. One day I found the courage to go up to a teacher, Miss K., to ask her to help me tell the time. Secretly, in registration, Miss K. would teach me how to tell the time and I learned this in about a week.

Thinking back, it was resourceful move of mine and took some confidence to ask for help. I was so pleased with myself. I told my mum I could tell the time and she bought me a gold watch. After that, I remember sitting in school and being able to tell the time. I was so proud.

I was desperate to learn. I wanted to sit at the front of the class. I was just not getting it; I wasn't understanding the way they were teaching me.

I remember struggling on the sports field, and PE and maths were my worst subjects. I hated netball, rounders and any team sports, where you had to be chosen. No one wanted to choose me to be on their team. The PE teacher would have to force someone to take me. I sometimes felt that even the girl who never ran would be picked before me. Imagine how that was for me, hearing 'we don't want her'.

I wanted to cry. I wondered why my parents brought me here, when we should have stayed in Ghana.

Back in the changing room, it was hell. They abused me, laughed at my trainers, at my leotard, cussed me for not hitting the ball or not catching it. Nobody should have gone through that; it was awful, daily and relentless.

At 16, I finished my exams and I did not do well. My only good grade was in home economics.

I showed my dad my results. He looked at them and said, 'Oh well, your life is over.' I remember thinking, 'So where do people go when their life is over? Where do they go?'

Looking back, maybe my dad had some of the same traits as me. When my parents met, my dad was studying law and he kept failing. He had really bad handwriting, he had obsessive compulsive traits – the toilet roll had to be in a certain way and in a certain colour – and he did not like change. I think maybe I have similarities with him.

My mum looked at the results, with disappointment in her face and said, 'Ah well, why don't you go and do catering as you are good with your hands?' I thought, 'She said I was good at something, I have never been told I was good at anything.'

I then did just that. I applied to Westminster College, was accepted and did a two-year Chef City & Guilds qualification.

Turns out, I am a pretty damn good chef! I qualified and got a job as a pastry chef and went to Switzerland to work there for a year. Then I worked at the Dorchester Hotel as a pastry chef for a year and a half. These were long hours for low pay.

Then a guy I was seeing said, 'Why did you not go to uni?' I said that people like me don't go to university and he queried, 'What you do you mean?' I continued, 'I am not very bright.' He disagreed, saying that when he first met me he thought I was bright and intelligent. I cried when he said these words, as I had never been told this in my life. The guy said we would fix this. He got me some forms and we started to complete them.

He applied to North London University for me, and I was given an unconditional place. I had to call my friend and ask him

what this meant. 'They want you, Alice. You can go anywhere,'
she said. So, I studied international hospitality management
as a four-year degree, including one year in training.

In my first year, I scraped through. In my second, I saw a
notice on the main noticeboard, 'Do you have problems
with spelling and remembering names?' There were other
questions too, and I answered yes to all of them. They booked
me an assessment and less than three hours later I was told,
'You will be pleased to know that you are severely dyslexic
and dyspraxic.' I thought, 'Why would I be pleased and
what the hell is this disease?' I was told, 'Don't worry about
dyspraxia, you will grow out of it.'

When I heard about this diagnosis, I remember asking my
tutor if I could leave my boyfriend now. I hadn't felt confident
to do my degree on my own. She said, 'Of course,' so I left
him and cried for England. So much crying, my pillow was wet.
I was angry at my parents for not realizing I had a learning
disability. Being teachers, they should have helped me. I was
crying as I felt I was not normal; I wanted to be like everyone.
I cried because I felt filled with shame. The diagnosis had
taken so long. I cried the whole night.

My support tutor told me of a support meeting that happened
every Thursday. I said I didn't want to go. I didn't want to mix
with disabled people. I wondered what they would look like.

I thought I wouldn't be able to relate to the other students,
but I reluctantly I went along and found this buzzing place

and we all just got on. I knew then that everything was going to be okay.

Still, I did not like me. There was a taboo in having a disability, even a 'hidden' one, and in Ghana, physically disabled people were shut away. They were always hidden, not integrated. People were not seen. However, being in the group meant I was enriched with feelings and emotions. Where were these coming from?

In the library at university there was a learning unit, with a Kurzweil machine. You could scan your books and it would read the book and play it back to you. I am an auditory learner, who struggles in lectures and finds it hard to listen and write at the same time, so I was given a grant to get a special computer and a dictaphone. These were great adjustments.

Besides the people who helped me, no one knew I was dyslexic, as I was still ashamed. When handing in coursework, I had to put a yellow sticker on my work. I waited until everyone had posted their stuff in the box, then put mine in afterwards, as I did not want anyone to know.

I was found out when we had exams and I was put in a separate room. So, when no one saw me, they would ask, 'Where's Alice?' I knew it was D day, so I confessed. 'I am in a separate room as I am dyslexic.'

'You are not dyslexic, you are intelligent,' some would say. I knew I would need to educate people again but I felt too tired to tell people about it.

Both my parents were alive when I graduated and they saw this happen. This was good for me. I wasn't doing it for them but I was pleased they witnessed it. I'm so grateful, too, for my friend who encouraged me to take this step.

I was still not okay with being dyslexic. If a black guy was interested in me, I would not tell him, as I thought he would run a mile. I had not come round to accepting my dyslexia. I thought it was a disease.

With help from Marcia, who coached me, my dyspraxia began to make sense. I thought about the way I struggled with swimming, driving, spatial awareness and how there always seemed to be so much going on in restaurants, all the noise, all the tickets, all the multi-tasking. I thought about my clumsiness and the long time I needed to process information.

Over time and with counselling, I have come to accept my dyslexia and dyspraxia and see them as a positive. My job as a chef is practical, I am doing things with my hands, enabling me to express my creativity. I see that the way I am is because of my dyslexia – in a good way. I am great at problem-solving and extremely empathetic. I am practical and pragmatic, able to 'think outside the box' and I am super-organized. I run my own business, a catering company.

Since 2020, I have been wearing my dyslexia as a badge

of honour. Within the first minutes of meeting people, I tell them I am dyslexic and I am proud of it. Often others reply by saying, 'I am too,' or, 'My brother is, as well.' It's as if this is a special club that not everyone can join.

My life has been hard but it has got better. I've worked out that if you have belief in yourself, others can believe in you and I'd like that to be my message to others.

‗‗‗

Alice Aggrey-Orleans, business owner and vegan private chef for an HNWI.

I've noticed parallels between being a black man and having dyslexia. They both are part of my identity; they're gifts I was born with. However, there are still many who would try to use these gifts against me. What they don't yet understand is that both have made me unstoppable.

Claud Williams, Founder of Dreams Nation, inspirational speaker and British Dyslexia Association ambassador.

Achieving the Dream as a Dyslexic Person

Solomon Smith

Society and the education system tend to isolate people like me, who have dyslexia. Life is full of obstacles and the challenge comes with pushing through them with all the strength and determination we have.

Being slow in the education system, I was deprived throughout my teens. I remember the feeling of living in fear and not having support. I left school with no GCSEs and, ever since, I've made it my will to test myself and be the light for people in my situation. When I felt isolated in my struggle, I decided my fear of this feeling would never stop me.

I attended Goldsmiths University, where I studied for a course in applied social science and youth and community. I pushed myself every day to complete all my work. The fear of being isolated again would not put me down. I finally achieved a degree and later a master's degree. This was one of the proudest moments of my life. I had finally turned my fear around; I was no longer the odd one out. My confidence was boosted!

I looked towards the future and thought, how could I not give back to my community after what I had achieved in life? I decided to start a charity, so that I could be the light for future generations. I wanted people to hear my story and believe that anything is possible in life, regardless of the difficulties you go through.

As a lifelong Brixtonian, I had identified the need for a space for homeless people, or any member of the public who needed us. My vision came to life when I founded the Brixton Soup Kitchen (BSK) in January 2013.

This was another proud moment for me. Seeing people smile gave me the strength to beat the odds, of avoiding homelessness when I was younger. I hated the fact that the homeless did not get enough support, which in turn affects the whole of humanity. Understanding all of this helped me hone my goals and acknowledge how the system works. This knowledge drove me to fulfil my dreams. BSK is a community space for homeless people as well as others less fortunate.

We aspire to provide food, drink and companionship, in a warm, friendly environment, on a daily basis.

Word of our great work and efforts has been spreading and we are receiving approximately 45 visitors a day, five days a week. We've served more than 10,000 meals, either eaten on site or distributed during food drop-offs and outreach sessions.

We have received much appreciated food donations from Pret A Manger, Greggs, Nando's, Satay Bar Brixton and Marks & Spencer. We have had media support from *The Voice* newspaper, Channel 4 and the South London Press, who awarded us the Our Heroes Award in April 2013.

At BSK, we have cherished trained professionals, who come in to deliver one-to-one consultation sessions with clients, to assist in re-housing, claiming applicable benefits and accessing back-to-work training. Including this training element is essential for me because I know how it feels to not be prepared for life's obstacles.

I really love my team at BSK. Teamwork is everything! We come together with a strong sense of love and unity, yet we are all from different backgrounds. The world is a platter of diversity which is ever growing. Respecting each other invites a cleaner environment. I want us all to take better care of the world.

We can all treat our problems as if they are infections and

find ways to cure them. Nothing changes, until you change your mind.

BSK will continue to provide a service for all. We will continue to invest in unity. We hope others will also be inspired to make happiness possible.

———

Solomon Smith, Founder and Manager Director of the Brixton Soup Kitchen.

" I am a black dyslexic but this doesn't define me. This is my superpower.

Some may say that being dyslexic causes me challenges but I use this as a positive.

This helps me think differently, have a positive mindset, show empathy, have a strong work ethic and give back to others.

My mind sometimes wanders but this is where my creativity starts. I get ideas for a project that grows into a great new initiative that can make a difference to others.

Let's embrace our superpowers and help change the narratives. Also, challenge decisions, speak out against injustice and be the best version of ourselves.

Never believe you are not worth it or don't belong. You are special, brilliant and more importantly worth it!

Akua Opong, Diversity & Inclusion advocate and STEM (science, technology, engineering and mathematics) ambassador.

24 How Dyslexia Changed My Life

Elizabeth Adjoa Marforwaah Takyi

When I was two years old, I left the UK for the other side of the world, Ghana, where both my parents were from. My mother is from Bekwai in the Ashanti region and my father from Japekrom in the Brong Ahafo region. A long way from my early life in Balham, South London.

The main thing I remember about school in Ghana was the struggle. No one spoke about dyslexia. If you didn't get something right, you got the cane and I experienced this pain and humiliation many times. A terrible way to treat a child.

The sad thing about this was that outside school, I was a playful child. I loved going out and being with my friends. I was creative with things and creative in outdoor play and I loved to explore. Even then, I was entrepreneurial and started selling things at a young age, helping my grandma on the market stall.

I cannot remember doing any homework though.

What really sticks out for me about school was at the end of the academic year and every half-term, there would be mini tests that we would have to sit. Everyone would get called up to admire their certificates and I would be left in the crowd, never winning anything. From the age of six years, until I returned to the UK at 12 years old, I can't remember ever receiving a certificate.

Besides getting the cane, if you got things all wrong, you would have to paint stones white or go and get the headteacher's shopping. Everyone would look at you thinking, 'Oh you are dumb, stupid and thick.' In Ghana, they would really bully children and call them names and that name would stick with you until you married and left the country.

I was always fighting in the playground to defend myself, in both Ghana and when I was back in the UK. I didn't understand why I could not pass these tests. However, I knew that I was not mad. Whatever anyone said to me, that much I knew.

I grew up in a family of five children and the rest of them all did well. Even now, my family see me as different and 'the black sheep'. I am outspoken but in Africa you're taught to be submissive and respectful. If an elder said something and I disagreed, I was told that I was rude. I have been labelled as rude so many times. I have even had fall-outs with my own family members because of my straight talking.

I feel that that I am possibly on the ADHD or autism spectrum, as I see things in a black and white way. I'm so straight talking and have such a short attention span but I've never undertaken any form of assessment. Even in the workplace, if someone annoyed me I would just tell them what I thought and walk away. As I become older, I am more patient, but I see these traits in my son, who has ADHD. He will just tell you straight if he does not like you.

Sometimes, I wonder, 'Who will I be today. Is it ADHD today, is it dyslexia, which one?' Sometimes I will be talking and it feels as if I've drifted off to another planet. That's the way I see it. I feel as if I have had enough of what's happening after two or three minutes and will drift away.

I would say I really struggled to read or write until the age of 15. Due to the continuous bullying by the other children, who would often ask what my problem was, I became very disruptive in class and was always getting in trouble with the teachers.

Eventually, I was excluded from school and, as a result, I ended up in the bottom set of the class and left school at

16, with all my GCSE grades labelled unclassified. I had no intention of ever going back to full-time education.

Despite this, I felt a lot of peer pressure to attend college with my friends and I managed to get onto a youth training scheme at a local college, to study hotel management. After a year on the course I left, puzzled about my learning skills but not yet knowing what was wrong. I worked as a receptionist for Yorkshire TV in London but was too scared to ask for a promotion as I felt incapable of reading, writing and spelling well enough. I had no support in the workplace and was ashamed to mention I had any difficulties to any employer. I kept it all to myself and suffered in silence, hopping from job to job when I felt I couldn't perform to the necessary standard.

Something in me still wanted to get a qualification and, in 2001, I was brave enough to enrol at South Bank University, London, to study human resource management and sociology. I did this even though I had doubts as to how I would embark on this journey, due to my inability to write essays and read effectively, and I also had two young children at the time. However, I wanted a better life for myself and my children. In my second year, when I was aged 32, I was referred for a dyslexia assessment at the Independent Dyslexia Consultants with David McLoughlin (chartered psychologist), based in Holborn, where I was eventually diagnosed with dyslexia, dyspraxia and Irlen Syndrome, which is where the brain struggles to make sense of the visual information it receives. This causes a variety of symptoms including visual distortions, physical symptoms like headaches, migraines, strain and fatigue, difficulty attending and problems with depth perception. I cannot cope with too much light. I get a lot of headaches and words seem to be moving on the page. At times, I have signed something without seeing certain words.

This diagnosis was a total shock to me. I now wondered what it would mean for my studies and how I would inform future employers and my family. I come from a Ghanaian background, where there is stigma attached to any learning difficulties and disabilities. However, with the support of the study skills team and one-to-one tuition, I successfully graduated with a 2:2. I later went on to study for my post-16 PGCE teaching certificate, at Greenwich University in 2014, with one-to-one support from a tutor, Tracey Partridge, who really believed in me, and helped and encouraged me to reach my full potential during my studies and future career.

I began teaching a subject specialism in TV and film media makeup and I loved this creative area. I also have qualifications in fashion styling, image styling for performance, creative hair styling, fashion photographic makeup and more. All of these increased my confidence and showed me I had abilities that I hadn't realized.

I thought I had finally found my passion and was free to teach what I really enjoyed but somehow I felt compelled to help other dyslexic people, who may be struggling within the education system or within the workplace. I couldn't forget everything I'd been through and wanted to help other people who might be suffering in the same way.

I realized that what had really helped me was the support of individuals, who mentored and held my hand as I worked my way through what my diagnosis meant and allowed me to find my self-belief.

This led to the start-up of my charity, Aspire2inspire (A2i) Dyslexia CIC (community interest company), and to where I am today, the founder and CEO of an amazing charity, as well as a qualified teacher for post-16 in special educational needs.

A2i's aim is to provide one-to-one support for adults and children with dyslexia and other specific learning difficulties who want to reach their full potential by identifying their skills and talents and utilizing them to the best of their ability. It's a wonderful resource and I hear every day about people we have helped and encouraged on their way.

————

Elizabeth Adjoa Marforwaah Takyi, entrepreneur, formerly the Founder and CEO of A2i – Dyslexia CIC, (Due to the increasing challenge of operating a small disability social enterprise in the current environment, the Directors of Aspire 2 inspire Dyslexia CIC (A2i's Dyslexia), have decided to close the community interest company, their last trading date was Friday 28th October 2022). Forbes featured, Advisory Board of Neurodiversity in Business, Genius of the Year 2021 runner-up, WAW 100 Most Inspirational Association 2019, BDA Smart Award 2019.

A poem by Ms Lyricist B 2021

Apprentice or master?

Am I a dyslexic apprentice or master creator?

I chose to choose the latter because I must.

I know I'll forever be learning, but my passion and my yearning, is to continue my belief and my own trust. My belief in my doing will be my conquering.

©**Jannette Barrett** aka Ms Lyricist B 2021, a proud dyslexic, author, poet and mental health awareness practitioner.

The Teenage Years

Ella-May Bria

I am 17 years of age and was assessed for dyslexia at the age of nine. I received an education, health and care plan aged ten years. The results found that I also have mild dyspraxia. I have known for as long as I can remember that I have these conditions because I was so young at the time of the assessment. I feel that they are a part of me and will not define who I am and what I can achieve in life.

I have a younger brother and sister. My mother is British-born of Nigerian heritage. My father is also British-born with Jamaican heritage. I am the only member of my immediate family with dyslexia. There is a theory that my late grandfather on my father's side could not read or write. However, he was an amazing painter and decorator. There is a strong possibility that he had undiagnosed dyslexia.

I have a wonderful seven-year-old Maltese Terrier dog, whom I adore. I think Mum bought him for me at the age of ten, to give me the confidence I needed, as well as something to talk about. My dog has definitely boosted my confidence; he is a celebrity in his own right and has more Instagram followers than I do!

The dyspraxia presented itself through having the challenges of learning to swim, skip and ride a bicycle. As a child, my mum always said that my mild dyspraxia was like small pinch of salt and that I could achieve if I practised enough. My parents were amazing and have offered me every way to gain confidence in these areas that most children would take for granted. I had private swimming lessons with Hayley, who was an amazing teacher. The one-to-one sessions were perfect for me. I learned to swim within one term. This gave me the confidence to participate in swimming at school, as well as at swimming parties with friends.

Every morning, Mum would take me downstairs to practise skipping in the kitchen and I was so chuffed when I managed to crack it! I learned to ride a bike almost by accident while on a school journey. There was something about being in an open space that gave me the balance and confidence I needed to ride.

As a teenager, my dyspraxia is evident when I am cooking. My wrist action is quite weak, so it takes me a while to complete tasks such as peeling potatoes and onions. My strategy with this is to keep practising and allow enough preparation time in the kitchen.

Having dyslexia has its advantages. I have the ability to think outside the box. I have a natural passion for creative media and editing audiovisuals. My dyslexia has helped me to use my imagination in creating content using a range of editing software. I also love to explore creative writing and often write in my spare time.

I have never been embarrassed about telling people that I have dyslexia. In fact, it has been really liberating because through conversations with others, I have discovered that so many other people are also dyslexic or dyspraxic, or indeed both. I have a love for reading; however, my main challenges continue to be with spelling and maths. I am fortunate that assistive technology has helped me to correct this and it is no big deal. I have an amazing maths and English tutor who is both kind and patient with me, which has really helped me to progress. I believe that dyslexic teenagers really benefit from the help and support of a tutor. Although there are a few instances to the contrary, mainstream education is unfortunately not designed to offer the time and resources for this learning challenge, and therefore, many of us are in danger of slipping through the net and not accessing the support we deserve.

I can be a quiet and reserved person at times, in social situations. Once I am familiar with people, I am a sociable and loyal friend. I also have a tendency to lose focus at times and can be easily distracted. I guess this is my creative brain in action! My friends have all been very supportive of me, and my dyslexia is not a barrier.

My advice for anyone who is like me is always to ask for help when you need it. Do not feel embarrassed. Dyslexia is no big deal. It does not define you as a person. Do not keep your dyslexia a secret. It is not shameful or negative. Society needs to adapt for you, not the other way around.

I recently had some exam feedback from my English teacher that my handwriting was messy. I politely informed him that I had tried my best but that my dyspraxia often contributes to this. He swiftly apologized and commended me on the quality of the work and understood that the focus should not be on the presentation.

My hopes and ambitions for the future are to be happy. I know that it will not involve being stuck in an office. I would love to work in editing for a supportive, neurodiverse-friendly, media production company. In the future, I plan to visit my old secondary school to share my journey and inspire other dyslexic teenagers to dream big and achieve. I do not see many other young dyslexic people of colour in UK media. I think this is a real shame, as we all need role models. The main celebrities have always been Richard Branson and Jamie Oliver. I am so pleased to be a part of this book to share my journey as a teenage British-born, African female with dyslexia.

———

Ella-May Bria, Media Creative – editing and post production. No social media links given.

" I often say I found my voice in words I couldn't spell. Because my exercise books in school always came back with red markings on them. I fell in love with poetry and began writing at the age of eight and didn't share any of my poetry with any one so they couldn't point out my spelling errors. I discovered spoken word poetry and since no one needed to see my writing on paper I started performing on stage, and that changed my life. I use poetry to express and make sense of the world around me and to highlight social issues.

Asma Elbadawi, a Sudanese-British spoken-word poet, activist, basketball player and coach. Successfully campaigned to get basketball governing body FIBA to allow wearing of the hijab.

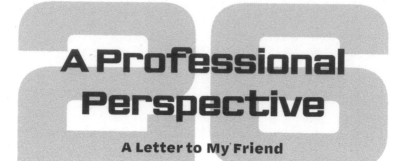

A Professional Perspective

A Letter to My Friend

Jannett Morgan

Dear Marcia,
When you asked me to contribute to your book, I was deeply honoured. I can't remember the exact moment when we went from two people connected by dyslexia (albeit in different ways) to two sistahs with a deep respect and affection for each other but I do know that I have become a far better person because of what I have learned from you. Your journey from a little girl let down by an education system that failed you to the 'neurodiversity narrative changer' (love that title) we see before us today is truly inspirational.

It may be hard for people to imagine how conversations about race were silenced, before Black Lives Matter forced even the most resistant of people to listen to what some of us have been saying for some time. I'd see people's eyes rolling in a *here-she-goes-again* way, or I'd watch people shifting in their seats because they felt so uncomfortable and couldn't wait for me to change the subject. This has had a huge impact on my career and the work I do now as a leadership consultant. As someone who is 'neurotypical', I wasn't sure at first if I should have a chapter in your book. It was our shared desire to change the narrative around dyslexia, particularly in relation to race and culture, that persuaded me to say yes. That and the fact that you're an extremely hard person to say no to! So, thank you for this opportunity to invite your readers to take a peek into our world.

My contribution to your book is through the professional lens of a Black specialist tutor, assessor and workplace coach but this is not just about my career. As you know, neurodiversity is something that runs throughout my personal story; for example, most people aren't aware that one of my sons is dyspraxic. Like many other parents, I had never heard of dyspraxia; I barely understood dyslexia before I started my training. And even though I was already a teacher, I struggled to say and do the right things to help my own child. I didn't receive the right information or support to help him thrive at school and despite the fact that he is an amazing man today, I still feel I let him down. I know many parents feel this way. In addition, based on representation in the media, dyslexia was something that didn't exist in the Black community (let's not even go there with dyspraxia). So, when I listen to you describe some of your experiences at school, as well as your professional life today, it resonates deeply with me.

Do you remember when we first met? It was at the Cultural Perspectives Committee event at the City of Westminster College, in 2017. What a night – I felt so connected to everyone in the space. We didn't speak very much at the time, so I didn't fully realize the powerhouse you were until much later. I just remember thinking, 'Finally, after years of looking for like-minded people, here is an event that focuses on the lived experiences of African and Caribbean children and adults with dyslexia and other specific learning differences.' I remember Asher Hoyles sharing her powerful story. She made us laugh, cry a little but most of all, Asher's story was one of triumph over adversity that we all needed to hear. I also recall the panel discussion at the end (I was thrilled to be invited to join the speakers on stage). The questions from the audience revealed the sense of frustration so many of us have felt when it comes to finding the right support. Assessments are expensive and sometimes the very people who are supposed to be on your side are the ones who create barriers.

But let's go back for a moment. Long before we met, I decided to switch careers and train as a teacher. I had completed my generic teacher training a few years before and was working in an FE college as a business studies lecturer. I first became aware of dyslexia in a real sense when I started delivering one-to-one additional learning support sessions for students on vocational courses. I wanted to understand why some students struggled with literacy and why conventional teaching and learning methods weren't working for them. That's what led me to study for my first specialist qualification: the Certificate in Adult Dyslexia Support. I will never forget my first student (a young, white, working-class male) and how empowered he felt when introduced to multisensory spelling strategies. This was the beginning of a lifelong commitment to working in the field of what we now call neurodiversity. The reason I think I've found dyslexia so fascinating is that I've never felt you have to be able to read to be 'intelligent'. I'd been a volunteer coach for the Hammersmith Reading Centre and worked with a brilliant Jamaican man who had basic/entry level reading and writing skills but had been a taxi driver for over 20 years and had put three children through university.

That said, when I started my course, my knowledge on dyslexia was pretty limited and leaned more towards the common stereotypes such as people with dyslexia *always* spell badly, often reverse letters and are not academic. Of course, that changed as I began to understand more about dyslexia. I learned about the social model of disability, which means that it is the environment that disables people (for instance, not allowing someone with limited working memory capacity to use a dictaphone). I began to see how positively students responded when exposed to dyslexia-friendly teaching and learning strategies. The irony was that while I was being told dyslexia exists in people from all backgrounds and all ethnicities, the more I studied, the more I realized that there was a lack of research about dyslexia in people who look like me!

After I left further education, I supported employees with dyslexia and worked in several London universities. During this time, I did another two years of postgraduate study that meant I was able to carry out post-16 diagnostic assessments – not easy! The challenges students experience in higher education can appear more subtle or may not become apparent until students are faced with trying to fit into an academic box that focuses on their weaknesses (one example being how to perform under exam conditions) instead of focusing on their strengths (coming up with original ideas, problem-solving).

My job in higher education involved conducting screening meetings with students who had indicators of dyslexia, referring for assessments and delivering one-to-one study skills tuition. A screening interview is often the first time someone gets to speak about their strengths and areas of difficulty in a safe, non-judgemental and informed setting. A 'positive' screening is required for a referral for assessment; if the assessment also turns out to be positive for dyslexia (and/or other specific learning differences), the student has a detailed report, with key recommendations for the support needed. It's a shame so much of my work has to be done in secret but it's a privilege to be trusted with people's hopes, fears and dreams and then be able to empower them to be successful on their courses.

Higher education is not for everyone but too many talented dyslexic students don't make it to university (or drop out) because they haven't received the right support earlier on. I remember you saying you didn't get your 'diagnosis' for dyslexia until you went to university. Sadly, many Black students are reluctant to seek help (even when they do get to university) until they find themselves in serious difficulty. Some of this is because of stigma within their communities but it is also because of the racist narrative about Black people and intelligence and the structural racism in the education system.

The dyslexia profession is made up of dedicated, caring, hardworking people but it is not immune to the structural racism that exists within the broader education system. Most practitioners and the people in leadership roles are white; this lack of diversity reinforces the narrative that dyslexia is a white and middle-class issue and further marginalizes students of colour. As a member of the Association of Dyslexia Specialists in Higher Education, I am expected to incorporate seven principles into my study skills work. One of the seven principles is 'Relevance', but for me, the importance of cultural relevance is rarely discussed. For example, dyslexic students from 'minority' backgrounds will often struggle to find research articles to support their brilliant ideas. You and I have spoken many times about the fact that Black children do not see themselves reflected in the school curriculum and when they do, it is mainly negative. You told me about your son and how learning Black history meant he could challenge what he and his peers were being taught but this was not well received by his teachers. If a young child is dyslexic, using culturally relevant materials is more likely to be engaging and memorable, and increase self-esteem and play to their dyslexic strengths. Alongside this, what typically works for dyslexic people will work for everybody.

Black students would come for their first study skills session with me and see a tutor who looked like them. I could see the shock, then the relief, then the joy on their faces – sometimes this happened in a couple of seconds but I saw it! I knew they were thinking something along the lines of, 'This woman will get it. She won't judge me; I won't have to go into lots of detail and she'll identify with my experiences. I can tell her anything and ask all my "silly" questions.' I would respond with empathy and compassion, validating their experiences, sharing identity stories (code switching into Jamaican, whenever the opportunity arose) and drawing on my cultural knowledge to help them translate their raw ideas into an academic format. Once this cultural foundation is established, it's much easier for students of any age to learn dyslexia-friendly strategies they can apply independently. To many dyslexic people, these strategies may not be obvious but when they begin to learn how to apply multisensory low-tech tools, such as highlighter pens or post-it notes, and high-tech resources, from reading and dictation software to mind-mapping software and mobile phones, their learning experience is transformed.

Over the years, we've talked many times about the fact that so little has been written about dyslexia in our community. This always made me mad because it means there is a one-sided picture of dyslexia. We've also talked about

how grateful we are to Asher and Martin Hoyles for their pioneering book, *Dyslexia from a Cultural Perspective*.
As a practitioner, I have shelves full of books on dyslexia, dyspraxia and autism but this was the first UK book to address ethnicity, race and culture (what we would now call an intersectional approach) co-written by a Black person about the Black experience. Yet, it was never on the reading list for any of the formal training courses I've completed. Why?!

Most of my work now is in the workplace, providing strategy coaching to dyslexic employees and advising employers on how to provide reasonable adjustments and, more importantly, create an inclusive environment for their employees. Many of the issues I've seen in education are similar to those in the workplace but many organizations are not designed with dyslexic employees in mind. I'm currently supporting a client of Caribbean heritage who refuses to disclose because she is worried about losing her job and is convinced her race is already a mark against her. I met her when I spoke at another community event and she reached out to me specifically because of the cultural connection. Without appropriate strategies to manage certain admin tasks, this client was experiencing more and more anxiety, trapping her in a vicious cycle. I have been able to show her strategies to organize her workload and manage her time in alignment with her thinking cycle, and suggest tips to manage her dyslexia-related anxiety. I say this because those of us who are practitioners do a lot of free extra-curricular work supporting our community family, who either aren't aware that 'established' organizations like the British Dyslexia Association exist, or they have legitimate concerns about trusting organizations, or they don't have the money to pay for services.

Of course, not all my clients and students are people of colour and I am just as committed to my white clients. In fact, one of the first things I do is signpost all clients, regardless of their background, to your wonderful LinkedIn posts. They all say how much they appreciate the positive affirmations and stories you share. That said, we know way too many Black children and young people who are still being excluded from schools. It has been reported that in 2018–19, Black children were found to be six times more likely to be excluded than their white peers in Cambridgeshire and five times as likely to be excluded in the London boroughs of Brent, Harrow and Haringey (McIntyre, Parveen, and Thomas, 2021). Many adults of African and Caribbean heritage are also struggling at work because of unidentified dyslexia or because they face double discrimination on the grounds of visible and hidden difference (this was evidenced in a report by the Westminster AchieveAbility Commission for Dyslexia and Neurodivergence in 2018). Having a cultural perspective means understanding how the environment can impact on and even disable people with dyslexia. It means providing person-centred support that takes their ethnicity into consideration and builds racial esteem to reduce the impact of covert and overt racism.

The other part of my work is leadership development, with a focus on the intersection of neurodiversity and race.

Leadership in the UK is often defined from a Eurocentric male and ableist perspective, so a Black woman with dyslexia is rarely represented as a leader. However, that's what you are, Marcia. I've been proud to sit beside you and others at the Dyslexia and SpLDs (specific learning difficulties) All-Party Parliamentary Group meetings, to ensure the experiences of Black people are at the centre of discussions and not an afterthought. I look forward to continuing our work with the British Dyslexia Association, to make changes at strategic level, including more diversity in leadership roles and a more inclusive curriculum for specialist teachers. This work is not about being popular and sometimes it's downright hard but we are joining up the dots and making change.

Finally, for now, do you remember when you said you found your voice? I knew at that point that there would be no stopping you. I love my job because I get to collaborate with amazing people like you and see the difference I can make. I know you're familiar with the Jamaican saying, 'Who feels it, knows it.'

While I'll never truly know what it's like to be dyslexic and I will never speak for someone who is dyslexic, the biggest compliment I've had is when people ask me if *I'm* dyslexic - it means I understand enough to be an advocate and a supporter.

So, please continue to wear your neurodiversity narrative changer crown with pride, my sistah, and know that I will continue to walk beside you.

I'll end this letter the way you end your messages to me:

Happiness!

From your colleague and friend, Jannett.

——

Jannett Morgan, dyslexia and dyspraxia specialist, delivering leadership programmes, coaching solutions and organizational consultancy.

"Think race, disability and intersectionality.

Melanie Hibbert, independent consultant in race, disability and intersectionality in the area of higher education and employment sector. Founder of the Intersectionality Network.

About the Editor

Marcia Brissett-Bailey was named as one of the Top 50 Influential Neurodivergent Women 2022 by Women Beyond the Box. I am a British Dyslexia Association (BDA) Adult Award Winner 2022.

Marcia is a passionate advocate and champion of dyslexia and neurodiversity, an advisory board member of the Centre for Neurodiversity Research at Work, a Neurodiversity in Business Co-production board member, and a judge panellist member of the Celebrating Neurodiversity Awards!

As a sought-after speaker, Marcia has shared her experiences and personal journey of dyslexia with various organizations, including Deloitte, Crown Prosecution Service, NatWest Group, Sparta Global, British Dyslexia Association, All-Party Parliamentary Group – Dyslexia and SpLD, and BBC London Radio.

Marcia is also a trustee at Waltham Forest Dyslexia Association, the co-founder of the British Dyslexia Association's Cultural Perspective Committee, and involved in various projects with the BDA around inclusion and diversity. Through this work, she hopes to enable others with a dis-ability to find their voice, especially from a cultural perspective.

Marcia is co-author in an anthology called *Pioneering Women Speak* and has also featured in several books: *Dyslexia from a Cultural Perspective, The Bigger Picture Book of Amazing Dyslexics and the Jobs They Do, Brilliantly Dyslexic* and *Reed Charitable Foundation Cookbook: Dyslexic Strengths and the Culinary Arts*.

Achieving a BSc (Hons) degree in information science with librarian status, a postgraduate qualification in career guidance, a certificate in person-centred counselling skills, a diploma in specialist teaching and an MA in special educational needs and disabilities, Marcia has worked in the education community sector for the last 30 years, providing information, advice and guidance in the higher education and post-16 sectors, as well as being a SEND lead.

Being level 3 IPSEA trained, Marcia is currently employed within a London based local authority as a special educational needs and disabilities information, support service case officer, to empower parents and young people with special educational needs.

As a qualified careers advisor, Marcia has a particular focus on personal development, helping young people to achieve their full potential and aspirations by setting personal goals.

She is fuelled by a passion to work with young people with dyslexic and neurodiverse needs in preparing for adulthood and transition to secondary school, college, university, the workplace or self-employment.

Marcia is keen to empower others to find their voice, working from a place of acceptance and self-love, which Marcia herself has had to invest in, in order to achieve, as she was always told what she could not do, rather than what she could.

Marcia is married and has two children and, over the years, has felt the need to 'hack the system', to develop mechanisms to navigate the education system and the workplace. She has learned to accept herself and realize that we are all different, in spite of the illusion that we are all the same shape and size and that there exists a dominant group within the human race.

Marcia has featured in the following articles and podcasts:

A2i Dyslexia: Topic: Generation Dyslexic from a Cultural Perspective: www.youtube.com/watch?v=e-IOPWZIakQ

Our Dyslexia Heroes Are Too White: Addressing Representation in Business with Marcia Brissett-Bailey: www.forbes.com/sites/drnancydoyle/2020/09/05/our-dyslexia-heroes-are-too-white-addressing-representation-in-business-with-marcia-brisset-bailey

Dyslexia is the New Black. Bearly Articulating is a disability inclusion think tank, with a mission to ignite conversations across the dimensions of ability. Interview with Marcia Brissett-Bailey: https://link.medium.com/NAqfSE9SVeb

Move Beyond Words, Episode 3: https://shows.acast.com/move-beyond-words/episodes/marcia-brissett-bailey

Maddie's Chat Show Podcast!!: 'Let's Talk Mental Health when You Are Dyslexic' (27): https://podcasts.apple.com/gb/podcast/maddies-chat-show-podcast

The Dyslexic Strength Podcast, by Tessa Pike. Episode #2 Spotify

"Growing up I knew there was something different about me, now I know dyslexia is my superpower but back then I was so frustrated that I could not read or spell properly. I found out I was dyslexic at the age of 40 when I was at university, it changed my life for the better and now I not only am I an author I also campaign to support others.

Sandra Carter CEO Director of Bodysymphony CIC, Kettorah and the NeuroVerse programme

Further Help and Support

Africa One Word Foundation (Nigeria): www.onewordafrica.org/onewordafrica

Amina Dyslexia Centre (Nigeria): https://aminadyslexiacenter.com/learn

Aspire2inspire Dyslexia (A2i) (UK): Due to the increasing challenge of operating a small disability social enterprise in the current environment, the Directors of Aspire 2 inspire Dyslexia CIC (A2i's Dyslexia), have decided to close the community interest company, our last trading date was Friday 28th October 2022.

Aspire2inspire Dyslexia (A2i) (UK), you can still find useful YouTube videos and Podcast online.

British Dyslexia Association: www.bdadyslexia.org.uk

CiPD: professional body for experts in people at work: www.cipd.co.uk/knowledge/fundamentals/relations/diversity/neurodiversity-work

Disability Rights UK: www.disabilityrightsuk.org

The Diverse Creative CIC: Neurodivergent: www.thediversecreative.org

Diversity and Ability (D&A): https://diversityandability.com

Do-IT Solutions: https://doitprofiler.com

Dyslexia Africa: www.dyslexia-africa.com

Dyslexia Alliance for Black Children:
www.dyslexiaallianceforblackchildren.org

Dyslexia Ghana: https://www.dyslexiaghana.com

Dyslexia Kenya: https://dyslexiakenya.org

Dyslexia Scotland: www.dyslexiascotland.org.uk

Genius within CIC: www.geniuswithin.org

The International Dyslexia Association: https://dyslexiaida.org

Jamaica Dyslexia Organisation:
https://www.jamaicadyslexiaassociation.com

Waltham Forest Dyslexia Association: https://wfda.org.uk

Books/Blogs/Articles/ Websites

Black and Dyslexic Podcast: https://podcasts.apple.com/us/podcast/ black-and-dyslexic/id1588272642

Charting Relations between Intersectionality Theory and the Neurodiversity Paradigm: https://dsq-sds.org/article/view/5374/4647

Hoyles, A. & Hoyles, M. (2007) *Dyslexia from a Cultural Perspective.* Hertford: Hansib Publications.

The Intersection of Race and Neurodivergence: 'The Black Dyspraxic' Shares on Overcoming Barriers: www.forbes.com/ sites/drnancydoyle/2020/08/07/the-intersection-of-race-and-neurodivergence-the-black-dyspraxic-shares-on-overcoming-barriers

Is Neurodiversity the New Black?: https://preciousonline.co.uk/is-neurodiversity-the-new-black

Neurodiversity: What Is It and What Does It Look Like Across Races?: www.open.edu/openlearn/health-sports-psychology/mental-health/ neurodiversity-what-it-and-what-does-it-look-across-races

No Time to Confront Racism in Neurodiversity: https:// blackgirllostkeys.com/adhd/no-time-to-confront-racism-in-neurodiversity

Our Dyslexia Heroes Are Too White: Addressing Representation in Business with Marcia Brissett-Bailey: www.forbes.com/sites/ drnancydoyle/2020/09/05/our-dyslexia-heroes-are-too-white-addressing-representation-in-business-with-marcia-brisset-bailey

A Reflection on Being Black and Neurodivergent: To Dismantle Racism and Ableism, We Must Address Intersectional Neurodiversity: https://thevarsity.ca/2022/02/20/being-black-and-neurodivergent

Twice as Hard: The Unheard Voices of Black Neurodivergent Employees in the Workplace. This report is presented and curated by The Diverse Creative CIC: https://www.thediversecreative.org. *Powered by Black Thrive & Impact on Urban Health*; https://blackthrive.org/about-us/

Where Are the BAME Dyslexic Role Models? Atif Choudhury: www.learningdisabilitytoday.co.uk/where-are-the-bame-dyslexic-role-models

Where Is the Research into Black Autism and ADHD?: www.openaccessgovernment.org/black-autism/91621

YouTube

Being Neurodivergent and Black – Vlog: www.youtube.com/watch?v=MhWE7mSWMUA

Black Men & Neurodiversity: www.youtube.com/watch?v=X_RhWexEgaE

Black Neurodiversity: The Intersectionality and Representation of Neurodivergence in the Community: https://elevateyoungminds.uk/blog/black-neurodiversity-the-intersectionality-and-representation-of-neurodivergence-in-the-community-6fe5p

Children of Colour with Autism Face Disparities of Care and Isolation: www.youtube.com/watch?v=aSomhokUlzo

Erin Manning on Neurodiversity, Black Life and the University as We Know It: www.youtube.com/watch?v=tYHSHRzj7eY

What It's Like to Be ADHD and Black: www.youtube.com/watch?v=oh-3ULQJiEY

Young, Gifted & Black with Autism: www.youtube.com/watch?v=Kjw-z8xBFE4

Research from Black perspective on dyslexia

UK

Camron, H.E. & Greenland, L. (2019) 'Black or minority ethnic' (BME), female, and dyslexic in white-male dominated disciplines at an elite university in the UK: An exploration of student experiences. *Race Ethnicity and Education*, 24(6), 770–788. https://eprints.whiterose. ac.uk/139655

Hoyles, A. & Hoyles, M. (2010) Race and dyslexia. *Race, Ethnicity and Education*, 13(2), 209–231.

USA

Dahmer, D. (2016) Changing the narrative around Black males and dyslexia. https://madison365.com/changing-narrative-around-black-males-dyslexia

Robinson, S.A. (2013) Educating Black males with dyslexia. *Interdisciplinary Journal of Teaching and Learning*, 3(3), 159–174. https://files.eric.ed.gov/fulltext/EJ1063059.pdf

About the Contributors

Alice Aggrey-Orleans, (UK) business owner and vegan private chef for an HNWI. LinkedIn: https://uk.linkedin.com/in/alice-aggrey-orleans

Ayana Bailey, (UK) CEO and Founder of Yani Creations, creative creator, actor and entrepreneur. www.yanicreations.co.uk

Gary Baron, (UK) MA in Child, Adolescent and Family Psychotherapy, PG Diploma in Psychosynthesis Counselling, Advanced Emotional Freedom Practitioner, NLP Diploma, Reiki Master, Diploma in Sandplay Studies, AAMET Registration, MBACP, UKCP Accredited Register. www.gbcounselling.co.uk, LinkedIn: https://uk.linkedin.com/in/gary-baron

Jannette Barrett, (UK) aka Ms Lyricist B 2021, a proud dyslexic, author, poet and mental health awareness practitioner. Facebook: www.facebook.com/jannette.barrett.71, LinkedIn: https://uk.linkedin.com/in/jannette-barrett-b58372126

Sabrina Ben Salmi, (UK) BSc Mother of the Year Award winner, author, ranked No.2 in the Pauline Long Show's 50 Most Inspirational Black Women in UK 2019. LinkedIn: https://uk.linkedin.com/in/sabrinabensalmi, Instagram: www.instagram.com/authorsabrinabensalmi, Facebook: www.facebook.com/sbensalmi

Ella-May Bria, Media Creative – editing and post–production. No social media links given.

Marcia Brissett-Bailey, (UK) listed as one of Women Beyond the Box's Top 50 Influential Neurodivergent Women 2022, author, narrative changer, Forbes featured, Co-founder of BDA Cultural Perspective Committee, WFDA trustee, Advisory Board Member of Centre for Neurodiversity at Work and Co-production Board Member Neurodiversity in Business. Instagram: theblackdyslexic, LinkedIn: Marcia Brissett-Bailey BSc, PG Dip (QCG), MA, IPSEA, Twitter: @ brissettbailey, Facebook: Dyslexia Talks UK, Marcia Brissett-Bailey – The Dots: https://the-dots.com/users/marcia-brissett-bailey-1209681

Karinna Brown-Williams, (UK) SEND Specialist Director and Consultant at Emerald SEND Consultancy. www.emerald-send-consultancy.com, LinkedIn: www.linkedin.com/in/Karinna-Williams

Dr Leonie Campbell, (UK) occupational and counselling psychologist. www.leoniecampbelltherapy.co.uk, www.psychologyforsuccess.co.uk

Sandra Carter, CEO Director of Bodysymphony CIC, Kettorah and the NeuroVerse programme.

William Carter, (UK) UC Berkeley PhD student, Fulbright Scholar, Bristol Politics BSc First Class with Honours, neurodiversity campaigner and public speaker. LinkedIn: www.linkedin.com/in/williamjamescarter

Atif Choudhury, (UK) Chief Executive, Diversity and Ability. https://diversityandability.com

Lucita ComWillis-Paul, qualified youth and community worker and educator. LinkedIn: https://uk.linkedin.com/in/lucita-c-p-33742720

Ruth-Ellen Danquah, (UK) neurodiversity consultant. https://ruth-ellen.com

Dee Davis, (US) dyslexia.funday@outlook.com

Antonia Douglas, cyber security professional and neurodiversity advocate. Passion for diversity and advancement of Black ethnic minority Women, in supporting them to pursue a career within technology. Instagram: https://www.instagram.com/p/CkvFcn7lj66/?igshid=MDJmNzVkMjY=

Winsome Duncan, (UK) book confidence coach, bestselling author and publisher. www.peachespublications.co.uk, LinkedIn: https://uk.linkedin.com/in/winsome-duncan-book-confidence-coach-

84622137, Instagram: www.instagram.com/peachespublications,
Facebook: www.facebook.com/peachespublications

Asma Elbadawi, (UK) Sudanese-British spoken-word poet, activist,
basketball player and coach. Successfully campaigned to get
basketball governing body FIBA to allow wearing of the hijab. www.
asmaelbadawi.com, Instagram: @asmaelbadawi

Chesney Ellis-Browne, (UK) Instagram: @the_gymbully

Natasha Gooden, (UK) choreographer, dancer, model and actor.
Instagram: @Natasha1gooden

Melanie Hibbert, (UK) independent consultant in race, disability
and intersectionality in the area of higher education and employment
sector. Founder of the Intersectionality Network. LinkedIn: https://
uk.linkedin.com/in/melanie-hibbert

LeDerick Horne, (USA) poet, speaker and disability rights advocate.
www.LeDerick.com, YouTube: www.youtube.com/c/LeDerickHorne,
Instagram: @LeDerick

Asher Hoyles, (UK) learning support practitioner, author and
performance poet. LinkedIn: https://uk.linkedin.com/in/asher-
hoyles-534900146

Oladoyin Idowu, (Nigeria) founder of One Word Africa. www.
onewordafrica.org, Instagram: @just_doyinn

Vivienne Isebor, (UK) Founder and Managing Director of ADHD
Babes, Clinical Associate in Psychology Trainee of East London NHS
Foundation, and performing artist. www.adhdbabes.com, LinkedIn:
https://uk.linkedin.com/in/vivienneisebor

Stefan Johnson, (UK) business owner and entrepreneur. Instagram:
sjcycleslondon, Facebook: SJ Cycles

Maxine Johnson, (UK) is a qualified Dyslexia Specialist Teacher
with over ten years of experience in this field. She currently works
in various schools and adult learning centres in London, carrying
out Exam Access Arrangements and dyslexia screening. Maxine also
tutors children/young people privately and is one of the Waltham
Forest Dyslexia Association's tutors working with children in the
primary and secondary sectors.

Dr Tracy Johnson, (USA) CEO and Founder of Vessels of Hope, President of Harcum College Alumni Association and Minister and Adjunct Professor. http://vesselsofhopevessels.org, LinkedIn: www.linkedin.com/dr-tracy-johnson-rockmore

Maddie Kamara, (UK) retail manager, entrepreneur, podcaster of *Maddie's Chat Show* and *Black Women's Corner*. www.listennotes.com/podcasts/maddies-chat-show-podcast-maddie-kamara, Instagram: www.instagram.com/maddiechatshow and @black_womanscorner

Rosalin Abigail Kyere-Nartey, (Ghana) Africa Dyslexia Organisation. https://africadyslexia.org, Facebook: www.facebook.com/RosalinKyere, Twitter: @RosalinKyere, LinkedIn: https://gh.linkedin.com/in/rosalinkyere

Angie Le Mar, (UK) British comedian, actor, writer, director, presenter and producer. Instagram: www.instagram.com/angielemar, LinkedIn: www.linkedin.com angie-lemar

Leslie Lewis-Walker, (UK) Senior People Lead at the UK Home Office. LinkedIn: https://uk.linkedin.com/in/leslie-lewis-walker-606424214, YouTube: https://youtube.com/user/taggthis

Zoe-Jane Littlewood, (UK) sports therapist, proud dyslexic, BDA Cultural Perspective Committee Member. LinkedIn: https://uk.linkedin.com/in/zoe-jane-littlewood-583147158, Instagram: www.instagram.com/the_dyslexic_movement

Dr Lauren McClenney-Rosenstein, (USA) Founder of Think Dyslexia, Orton-Gillingham specialist A/AOGPE. https://thinkdyslexia.org, LinkedIn: www.linkedin.com/company/think-dyslexia-llc, Instagram: @thinkdyslexia

Laura Mohapi, (UK) multidisciplinary artist with predominant interest in societal structures and human wellbeing, Founder of Head Of A PinCIC. www.lauramohapi.com/hisen, Instagram: @laura.mohapi

Jannett Morgan, (UK) dyslexia and dyspraxia specialist, delivering leadership programmes, coaching solutions and organizational consultancy. LinkedIn: https://uk.linkedin.com/in/jannett-morgan

Claud K. Mudimbe, (USA) facilitating class action settlement recovery for the Fortune 500 and more in the Argent Settlement Bay Area. Instagram: @power_by_dyslexia

Eniola Oluwasoromidayo, author of Rise book https://linkedin.com/in/eniola-oluwasoromidayo

Alex Onalaja Jr, (UK) featured on Forbes, named in the top 50 inspiring, prominent and influential voices in UK Black Tech by Tech Nation, entrepreneur, author, speaker, mentor, Black dyslexic, contributor at Global Business Playbook. LinkedIn: www.linkedin.com/in/alex-onalaja, Instagram: @wersuccessors, Twitter: @tkonalaja

Akua Opong, (UK) Diversity & Inclusion advocate and STEM (science, technology, engineering and mathematics) ambassador. LinkedIn: https://uk.linkedin.com/in/akua-opong

Craig Pinkney, (UK) criminologist and urban youth specialist, PhD researcher and Director of Solve Online Learning Centre. LinkedIn: https://uk.linkedin.com/in/craig-pinkney-18830a44

Remi Ray, (UK) neurodivergent high-performance coach, one of Women Beyond the Box's Top 50 Influential Neurodivergent Women 2019, entrepreneur, creative business strategist, programme curator and Founder of The Diverse Creative CIC. www.thediversecreative.org, Instagram: @iamremiray, LinkedIn: https://uk.linkedin.com/in/remiray

Jeannette Roberes, MEd (US) Chief Academic Officer Bearly Articulating, speech therapist and dyslexia advocate. www.bearlyarticulating.com, LinkedIn: www.linkedin.com/in/jlrwashington, Instagram: Bearly Articulating @bearly_articulating

Roger Robinson, (UK) TS Eliot Ondaatje Prize-Winning Poet, Follow of the Royal Society of Literature, alumnus of The Complete Works, collaborator on The Rest Residency, and musician. https://rogerrobinsononline.com

Makonnen Sankofa, (UK) organizer of *The Black Books Webinar*, author and radio presenter. LinkedIn: https://uk.linkedin.com/in/makonnen-sankofa-b5a709218, Instagram: @makonnen.sankofa

Rod Shields, (UK) business owner, property developer and pre-teen entrepreneur who sold a number plate at 18 years old and bought a three-bed semi to become a landlord. Loves start-ups and thinking outside the box. LinkedIn: www.linkedin.com/rod-shields, Instagram: www.instagram.com/blandlord

Solomon Smith, (UK) Founder and Manager Director of the Brixton Soup Kitchen. Instagram: www.instagram.com/brixtonsoupkitchen, LinkedIn: https://uk.linkedin.com/in/brixtonsoupkitchen

Keisha Adair Swaby, (UK) international inspirational speaker, dyslexia speaker, Radio Diamond presenter, Executive Member of Jamaicans Inspired, certified Les Brown Speaker, neurodiversity advocate, named as one of Women Beyond the Box's Top 50 Influential Neurodivergent Women 2022, Founder of Empowering Dyslexics. Instagram: @keisha.swaby

Elizabeth Adjoa Marforwaah Takyi, (UK) entrepreneur, formally the Founder and CEO of A2i – Dyslexia CIC, Forbes featured, Advisory Board of Neurodiversity in Business, Genius of the Year 2021 runner-up, WAW 100 Most Inspirational Association 2019, BDA Smart Award 2019. A2i – Dyslexia CIC, closed the community interest company, and last trading was October 2022. Twitter and Instagram: @A2idyslexia

Onyinye Udokporo, (UK) CEO and Founder at Enrich Learning, EdTec entrepreneur, educator, public speaker, author, pioneer of social mobility, ranked as one of the Top 150 Future Leaders by Powerful Media in partnership with HSBC and the University of Oxford. www.enrichlearning.co.uk, LinkedIn: www.linkedin.com/today/author/onyinyeudokporo, Instagram: @Onyinye.udokporo

Claud Williams, (UK) Founder of Dreams Nation, Inspirational Speaker and British Dyslexia Association ambassador. https://dreamnation.co/who-is-claud-williams, Linkedin: https://uk.linkedin.com/in/claudw

Brin and Nial Wilson, (USA) LinkedIn: www.linkedin.com/in/delano-wilson, Instagram: @delan_macs

Winifred A. Winston, (USA) advocate, trusted advisor, bestselling author and founder of the *Black and Dyslexic Podcast*. www.soallcanread.org/b-a-d-podcast.html, LinkedIn: www.linkedin.com/in/winifredwinston-dei-neurodiversity.

Sandra Iris Wolo, (UK) Founder and CEO of Africa Dyslexia United (UK and Congo), also known as Adult Dyslexics Unit. Instagram: @adultdyslexicsunited

References

ACAS (2019) *Neurodiversity in the Workplace.*

Blakis, B. (2021) *Black Neurodiversity: The Intersectionality and Representation of Neurodivergence in the Community.* https://elevateyoungminds.uk/blog/black-neurodiversity-the-intersectionality-and-representation-of-neurodivergence-in-the-community-6fe5p

Illingworth, K. (2005) 'The effects of dyslexia on the work of nurses and healthcare assistants.' *Nursing Standard.* 19(38), 41–48.

McIntyre, N., Parveen, N. & Thomas, T. (2021) Exclusion rates five times higher for black Caribbean pupils in parts of England. *The Guardian,* 24 March, 2021. https://www.theguardian.com/education/2021/mar/24/exclusion-rates-black-caribbean-pupils-england

Michail, K. (2010) *Dyslexia: The Experiences of University Students with Dyslexia.* Thesis submitted to the Faculty of Education Of The University of Birmingham For the degree of Doctor of Philosophy.

(2018) *Neurodiverse Voices: Opening Doors to Employment.* Loughton: The Westminster AchieveAbility Commission for Dyslexia and Neurodivergence.

(2021) *Neurodiversity in the Criminal Justice System: A Review of Evidence.* HM Inspectorate of Prisons.

Opitz, B., Schneiders, J.A., Krick, C.M. & Mecklinger, A. (2014) Selective transfer of visual working memory training on Chinese character learning. *Neuropsychologia,* 53(1), 1–11. https://doi.org/10.1016/j.neuropsychologia.2013.10.017

Sturge, G. (2021) *UK Prison Population Statistics 2021*. London: House of Commons Library.

Von Károlyi, C., Winner, E., Gray, W. & Sherman, G.F. (2003) Dyslexia linked to talent: Global visual-spatial ability. *Brain and Language*, 85(3), 427–431. https://doi.org/10.1016/S0093-934X(03)00052-X

World Federation of Neurology (1968) *Report of Research Group on Dyslexia and World Illiteracy*. Dallas, TX: WFN.

INDEX